4TROOPS
★ ★ ★ ★
THE MISSION IS MUSIC

4TROOPS
★ ★ ★ ★
THE MISSION IS MUSIC

FORMER CPT.
MEREDITH MELCHER

FORMER SGT.
DANIEL JENS

STAFF SGT. (RET.)
RON HENRY

FORMER SGT.
DAVID CLEMO

Newmarket Press • New York

FIRST EDITION
10 9 8 7 6 5 4 3 2 1

ISBN: 978-1-55704-947-6 (paperback)
ISBN: 978-1-55704-948-3 (hardcover)

Library of Congress Catalog-in-Publication Data available upon request.

QUANTITY PURCHASES
Companies, professional groups, clubs, and other organizations may
qualify for special terms when ordering quantities of this title.
For information, email sales@newmarketpress.com or write to
Special Sales, Newmarket Press, 18 East 48th Street, New York, NY 10017;
call (212) 832-3575 ext. 19 or 1-800-669-3903; FAX (212) 832-3629;.

SPECIAL THANKS TO:
Project Writer Diana Landau
Designer Timothy Shaner at Night and Day Design (nightanddaydesign.biz)

Produced by Newmarket Press: Esther Margolis, President and Publisher;
Frank DeMaio, Production Director; Keith Hollaman, Executive Editor;
Paul Sugarman, Digital Supervisor

Manufactured in the United States of America

www.newmarketpress.com

Contents

Introduction
A New Mission

As the year 2010 unfolded, Americans discovered and took to their hearts a new and unusual musical group. 4TROOPS are U.S. Army combat veterans—three young men and one woman who served on the front lines in Iraq and Afghanistan. While they were overseas, music played a crucial and very personal role in all their lives. They would sing at everything from large military events to jam sessions in the barracks after a long day in the field, briefly transporting themselves and their buddies home. They also lent their voices to somber occasions like memorial services, where they would sing to remember those who had been lost.

Now these four have come together for a singular purpose: to sing on behalf of all troops, to honor their sacrifices, and to create awareness of their needs.

The members of 4TROOPS—Former Cpt. Meredith Melcher, Former Sgt. Daniel Jens, Staff Sgt. (Ret.) Ron Henry, and Former Sgt. David Clemo—have been singing all their lives. When they joined the Army, each became part of a long and distinguished tradition of soldiers making music for each other, a history going back to Irving Berlin writing shows for troops to perform in World War I, and even further. Now, though, the sense arose that a group of singing soldiers could move into the pop-music mainstream—given the right combination of talent, direction, and timing. A few entertainment-world visionaries at DSW Entertainment, a management company, and the Sony Music Entertainment MASTERWORKS record label believed the time was right and set things in motion.

Our national mood today, unlike several decades ago, is one of profound gratitude to U.S. servicemen and -women, who have served faithfully through the two current wars. Alex Miller, Sony MASTERWORKS' general manager, tells of meeting a man in Santa Fe who had just learned about 4TROOPS from an NPR broadcast. "He'd been in Vietnam, class of '68," a time when returning troops weren't feeling the love. "Back then we couldn't separate the war from the warrior. But now we're getting better at recognizing that we have to take care of our own. We see veterans in need on the streets of New York, and we know it's not right."

Even though we may feel an obligation to our military and veterans, we haven't always lived up to it. With this as the backdrop, DSW and Sony Music asked, "How can music help?" 4TROOPS was born out of the desire to say thank you to the current generation of veterans and serving military, to make the rest of us more aware of their challenges, and to help heal their hearts with music.

Music is so often the way we express our deepest emotions and aspirations—think of Marian Anderson singing at the Lincoln Memorial or the tradition that sprang up after 9/11 of singing "God Bless America" at ball games. For the members of 4TROOPS, this was the chance of a lifetime to do what they all felt deeply called to do, while making a difference in the lives of other veterans. Meredith Melcher says, "Every troop, no matter where they've been or what they've done, has a story to tell. It could be a story of courage or loss or brotherhood. And for us this opportunity is so unique because we get to share our stories through music." For David Clemo, "The best part of this whole project is the positive feel behind it. It's not politically tricky. It's us saying, we understand what you're going through, and bringing it across to civilians who might not understand." He goes on, "Sometimes people aren't sure how to say thank you. Hopefully, we can bridge the gap."

From the start, 4TROOPS' mission has been nonpolitical and nonpartisan. "For them it's always been about the warrior, not the war," says Alex Miller. "I think it's one reason why they are being accepted from all sides. One thing we agree on is that American fighting men and women are doing a job on our behalf—and that as veterans they deserve to lead a rich life without the struggles so many experience."

> We get to share our stories through music.
>
> —MEREDITH MELCHER

Marcus Hummon, who loves 4TROOPS' version of his song "Bless the Broken Road," puts it this way: "Even those opposed to the current wars welcome the opportunity to show support for the troops; that we worry and pray for and are proud of them. I think 4TROOPS gives us a way to focus that unifying energy."

This book tells the story of how the group formed and its astonishing ascent. In just a few short months, guided and supported by DSW, Sony Music, and their committed team of coaches, producers, engineers, and of course their own families, the 4TROOPS came together, learned to sing as a seamlessly blended unit, recorded a top-selling CD, and took their new act on the road. Their mission of music has already reached millions and touched the lives of veterans, in part through donations made from sales of their CD to veterans' groups. It's a great American story. Please welcome . . . *4TROOPS!* ★

One time in Iraq I was playing my guitar out in the hall, and the next thing I knew almost my entire battery was surrounding me and having a good old time. It made me feel really good that I could do that. There's something about soldiers being at war that just takes things to a whole new level of closeness, so to be able to provide that service . . . it's just a nice break in a place like that. Kind of a light out of the darkness.
—DANIEL JENS

Part 1
BASIC TRAINING

The Journey Begins

In the autumn of 2009, four U.S. Army veterans of the Iraq and Afghanistan wars were finding their way in the world . . .

★ *Former Captain Meredith Melcher*, 29, who led a medical ambulance platoon evacuating wounded soldiers in the early days of Operation Iraqi Freedom, had been working in corporate America after four years in the Army, and had just started graduate school in Virginia to study to become an English teacher.

★ *Sergeant Daniel Jens*, 36, looked forward to heading back home to Wisconsin from his last posting at Fort Hood, Texas, after four years of duty. Though starting to build a career in music and leading worship at his church, he thought a lot about the friends left behind who still faced combat.

★ *Staff Sergeant Ron Henry*, 41, had just completed twenty years of active duty in the Army's Transport Division at Fort Eustis, Virginia, where he sang with a group on base known as the Transportation Express. He was making music at church and had cut his own CD.

★ *Former Sergeant David Clemo*, 30, had finished seven years in the Army in 2008, including serving as a communications specialist with the Airborne Corps in Afghanistan and Iraq, and then helping direct the U.S. Army Soldier Show for three years. He had recently landed a job as a cable technician in the Arlington, Virginia, area.

One day in mid-November, Jens noticed a message in his email inbox from someone in New York, asking if he'd be interested in helping to form a patriotic-themed pop vocal group. "I thought it must be spam," Daniel says—maybe from someone who had seen him

Former Captain Meredith Melcher　　　*Former Sergeant Daniel Jens*

perform the previous year on the show *America's Got Talent* and was putting him on. There had been plenty of crank comments posted on the show's website after his appearances, along with high praise.

But the emails, from an artists' management company called DSW Entertainment, kept coming, and eventually Daniel called back. What he heard in that first conversation with David Simoné and Winston Simone took a while to really sink in. They liked Daniel's singing and agreed with *America's Got Talent* host Piers Morgan, who said that he had "plenty of charisma and appeal." DSW was working with Sony Music to put together a group of singers who had served their country. They figured there must be a lot more talented singers who had recently served in America's armed forces, at least a handful of whom could be recruited for a successful pop vocal group, and they believed American audiences would warmly embrace such a group. With recognition growing that our troops would be fighting in overseas wars for some time ahead, then coming home to an uncertain economic future, veterans organizations and others were mobilizing to offer ongoing support and emotional sustenance. So, would Daniel have any interest in being the first recruit? And could he help to round up some others?

It didn't take long for the two DSW partners (who aren't related, despite their similar last names) to convince Jens of their bona fides: their background as recording label executives, managers, and producers has included working with some of the biggest names in the music industry, from Elton John to Bon Jovi to David Geffen. This project was being done hand in hand with Sony Music. Daniel was interested beyond any doubt—since appearing on *America's Got Talent*, he had continued to perform at military and veterans' events whenever the chance came along. "Any time I could lift up the spirits of my fellow soldiers by singing and playing guitar for them, it always made me feel really good," he says.

What about finding other military voices with top-shelf talent who could make such a commitment? Jens didn't see himself as having those resources. But he knew whom to call. Victor Hurtado, currently Production Director of the U.S. Army Soldier Show, is a former Army soldier himself, as well as a songwriter, manager, and "the William Morris Agency for performing troops, as I sometimes call myself," he laughs. Daniel had been referred to Victor by Nigel Caaro, an *America's Got Talent* producer who said, "Look after him"—and Victor took all such assignments seriously. As part of his informal placement service for talented vets, he kept a database of MP3 files, videos, performing bios, and so on. He'd already gotten Daniel a few gigs, including a charity show for wounded veterans in Oakland, Florida, an event benefiting Habitat for Humanity.

Former Staff Sergeant (Ret.) Ron Henry

Former Sergeant David Clemo

When Jens finally reached Hurtado, he conveyed the importance of contacting the DSW team, which his mentor did that very evening.

"It was such an organic conversation," Hurtdo says, "unbelievably so. What kind of a group should it be? How many people? What's the repertoire? We went through a lot of possibilities, but they didn't impose any need to make all those decisions right away." Over the years Hurtado had been approached by many promoters wanting to use military personnel in dubious endeavors—but he quickly became convinced that DSW had serious intentions and the right motivations. "David and Winston are major players in the industry, but they more or less left it up to me to present some prospects."

So Hurtado opened his Rolodex and started making calls. Over the years he had guided scores of young performers through stints in the Soldier Show (see page 73), and nothing could have been better preparation for this assignment. "I'd worked with so many different people and different voices," he notes. "The Soldier Show is like the five-hundred-pound bench press for your chops as a producer." He had the sense of what it takes to put together a successful mainstream act: consistency of tone, professionalism, voices that work together in harmony but can also stand out on a solo basis.

> What kind of a group should it be? How many people? What's the repertoire?
>
> —Victor Hurtado, Associate Producer

It took him very little time to arrive at two names with Soldier Show credits: Former Captain Meredith Melcher and Former Sergeant David Clemo. He had good footage of both, which he sent on to DSW.

"I thought of Meredith right away," he says. "She's like a singing machine but with tremendous heart and an amazing range. I knew she had just started at grad school but I was hopeful." Even though Melcher had taken pragmatic steps toward a career outside music, she still cherished the dream, and agreed to put school on hold for a bit.

"When I reached David," Victor continues, "he told me, 'I just got a job with the cable company.' But I thought he could really be catalytic for the group. He has that beautiful high pop voice, and he would also understand the toils involved, set an example of fortitude." Not only had Clemo just found a civilian job, he'd just found out that his fiancée, Joann, another Soldier Show alum, was pregnant. But this is how it's been for him, he says: "Every time I try not to do music, it's almost as if it finds me. At this point I don't put anything out of reach."

For Melcher, "It was encouraging to hear that Dave would be in the group. He's one of the best male singers I've ever met, so I knew right away that I'd be able to work well with him."

The DSW team had embarked on the project with few preconceptions about what the group should be. "Let's say we could have had it all," says Winston Simone, "in which case maybe there would have been a member from each branch of the service." It quickly became clear that this was impractical, and there were other diversity issues to consider. For instance, the idea that women should be represented didn't occur to them until a bit later, "but the reality is that women are all over the military now," says Simone. And once they saw and heard Former Captain Melcher, it was a done deal.

It also seemed right that African-Americans, so prominently represented in the armed forces, should have a presence in the group. Again, Hurtado turned to his Army Entertainment contacts. Well acquainted with the huge talent and personality of Staff Sergeant Ron Henry, he thought of Ron right away—except he believed that Ron was still on active duty, and the singers needed to be vets. But a short while later Hurtado got a wonderful surprise when he discovered that Henry had in fact retired. He quickly edited together some footage of Ron performing and being interviewed and sent it to DSW. They immediately said: "That's our guy!"

Now there were four. Four strong, individual voices with the potential—so they and their supporters believed—to meld together in the crucible of rehearsing and performing and create a "chemical infusion," as Ron Henry puts it. Four combat veterans recently separated from the fellowship of the Army, still feeling deeply tied to their comrades in the service and excited by the prospect of using their talents to help those comrades and their families however they could.

> Every time I try not to do music, it's almost as if it finds me.
>
> —DAVID CLEMO

All very well in theory. But as Winston Simone points out, "none of this was going to work at all if they weren't good. They couldn't just be four actors who could lip-synch to music. At the end of the day, David and I had to look each other in the eye and know this group was valid on its own terms, and up to the task."

That was about to be put to the test, but one key step remained at the start of the journey: finding a name that would truly reflect the essence and intent of the group. Four soldiers, four singers. Singing for their fellows, for the troops. "We all brainstormed it," recalls Daniel Jens. "Writing words on cards, shuffling them around, talking it over for several days." It was Jens, finally, who hit on the idea of using the numeral "4" as a play on words. "For the troops." **4TROOPS**. ★

Roll Call

Former Captain
Meredith Melcher

"**The call from Victor came** very much out of the blue," says Meredith Melcher about the momentous invitation to come to New York and audition for a new group—the soon-to-be-called 4TROOPS. "Victor has a tendency to sound really excited, so at first I wasn't sure how big a thing this might be. But when he mentioned Sony Music, it made my ears prick up.

"Then after I'd talked with DSW on the phone and learned about the people they'd worked with, it became clear what a big deal it was."

It was vintage Meredith: low-key, deliberate, but ultimately ready to follow music almost anywhere. Now twenty-nine, former Captain Melcher was born at Fort Ord, California, and lived the childhood of an Army brat. Her father, David F. Melcher, is a retired Lieutenant General and her mother, Marla, was a dedicated Army spouse for more than thirty-two years. Among the places the Melchers called home when Meredith was a child were Alaska, West Point, and California.

Dave Melcher saw early signs of his daughter's musical talent. "She sang in the car all the time, would run through a huge repertoire, and did school musicals, but she really blossomed during piano lessons," he recalls. "She learned theory fast and has great pitch; she can play anything by ear." In high school she joined choirs, and at the College of William and Mary, where she graduated in 2002, she sang with and eventually led an accomplished a cappella group called The Accidentals.

While Meredith's undergraduate career was broadly academic, she went to William and Mary on a four-year ROTC scholarship. Her father hadn't pushed her in that direction, "but she fell in with such a bright, engaging group of young people," he recalls. "So she decided to stay with it." After completing her first year in ROTC, Meredith realized she loved the program, "which was essentially four years of tactical Army training as well as leadership instruction," and never looked back. "I also knew that it would mean a good, solid job after graduation, and it would give me life skills I would need to be successful in the civilian world: responsibility, accountability, leadership, organization, discipline."

The start of Meredith's senior year coincided with 9/11. "I had just returned home from the morning's physical training session, and saw it on the news. But it didn't even dawn on me at the time that the events of that day would later be the cause of my deployment to Iraq."

While an ROTC cadet, Meredith elected to join the Medical Service Corps because she thought the job would translate readily to civilian life. "We're basically healthcare operations officers, the war planners of the medical branch," she says. In simplest terms, that means organizing, deploying, and tracking all medical assets, including personnel, equipment, and ambulances. She went through the MSC Officer Basic Course from July to September 2002, then headed to Fort Hood, Texas, for her first assignment as an Ambulance Platoon Leader. "After being on the job for about three months, I got word that we would likely be heading to Iraq."

Like all soldiers, Meredith had committed to serve where and when she was assigned; for her this meant being deployed as a young lieutenant to Kuwait in February of 2003, in preparation for the launch of combat operations. Attached to the Third Infantry Division, her unit (the 546th Area Support Medical Company) crossed into Iraq a day after major combat operations commenced. "Our initial push was fast and furious, and there were no roads to travel on; we simply crossed desert sand," she recalls. "The dust got so bad you couldn't even see the vehicle in front of you in the convoy, and we would often crash into one another. We actually had to ditch an ambulance on the side of the road." But they made it north through Baghdad to Balad and established the first troop medical clinic at what became Logistical Support Area Anaconda. The ambulance platoon Melcher led successfully evacuated hundreds of injured Americans and Iraqis to higher levels of medical treatment.

Above: *Meredith, age two.* Right: *Meredith got involved in music at an early age.* Opposite: *The Melchers are a proud military family with over thirty-eight years of combined active-duty experience. Left to right: Dave, Meredith, Marla, and younger daughter Katie as a West Point cadet.*

"I had to grow up fast," she says. Although she was spared from direct contact with the enemy, "I saw a lot of wounded Americans and Iraqis, and some of the dead as well, so that was a little harrowing." Some days were harder to get through than others, and Melcher thinks this is true for anyone serving around combat. "We're all a little bit scared, so we're going to use whatever we can to get through it, whether that's music, whether that's humor, whether that's just sitting down together to talk about what you're seeing each day."

I had to grow up fast . . . I saw a lot of wounded Americans and Iraqis.

One verse of "For Freedom," 4TROOPS' powerful single, tells of a young woman joining the service and her parents' reaction: "And for freedom they'll let her go." Melcher's parents experienced the full range of emotions with their daughter on duty in a war zone. "My dad, being a career officer, got it," Melcher says. "He understood that it was about going to do a mission, a job, whereas my mom was extremely emotionally affected." Communications from Iraq were sporadic during the early weeks of the campaign, and she thinks "that might have been better for

my mom than being able to talk all the time. I'd call her maybe every couple of weeks or so. I wish I could have eased her pain more."

Ultimately Melcher spent four years on active duty, but her Army service took a sharp turn just weeks after returning from deployment in late 2003. She'd had few chances to sing while overseas, except in a July Fourth talent show and once when a small Army rock ensemble came to perform in Balad. She knew about the Soldier Show, however, and "made it crystal clear to my chain-of-command that I had every intention of trying out." With their full support, she went through the arduous audition process, and as a member of the 2004 show performed for audiences of more than 100,000 military personnel and civilians worldwide.

"Being in the Soldier Show helped me find my own voice," Melcher says. "It gave me the skills I needed to become a good performer—to really put on a show and get the audience motivated and entertained. It certainly helped with my vocal ability. I got to know my strengths and weaknesses, and how to work with them."

Performing in the show also gave Melcher an early taste of the power of entertainment to salve the emotional wounds of deployment, for both soldiers and families. Because it was 2004, when the war was relatively new, many of those in the audiences had family overseas or had just returned themselves, she notes. "We would have meet-and-greets with audience members after the shows, and so many would come up and say 'I can't believe what I just heard . . . it seemed like you were singing to me and my family.' Now we're having similar experiences with 4TROOPS."

Through the show, Melcher also formed two friendships that were crucial in the birth of 4TROOPS: with Director Victor Hurtado and with fellow singer David Clemo. She and Clemo have become duet partners and fast friends, touring together while promoting the group's concert film *Live from the Intrepid* at PBS stations around the country. Because they're so tight, they can give each other a hard time: Clemo jokes that it's been much better being reunited with Melcher since they left the Army "because now I don't have to salute her."

Opposite: *Then-Lieutenant Melcher and her platoon preparing to deploy.* Above: *Melcher entertains at the piano at Camp Doha, Kuwait, in 2003.*

As a Former Captain, Melcher held the highest rank among members of the 4TROOPS, and her leadership qualities are still evident during their current adventures on the road. Those traits also factored into Hurtado's reaching out to her when he was asked to recruit ex-Army singers for the prospective group. "She was always so consistent and responsible and professional in how she came at it, and I knew that would serve her well in this new experience," he says. Melcher does take pride in her approach to work of any kind. "I always try to come with my 'A' game," she says simply.

But all that still lay in the future when Melcher was honorably discharged in 2006. Her pragmatic streak argued against trying to make a career in music—especially after she followed a whim and tried out for *American Idol* one season. "I did it mostly on impulse. It didn't go well! I think nerves got the best of me." By then she was already working at the first of several jobs in corporate America. Feeling the need for a more fulfilling career, she settled on teaching: in 2009 she was accepted at graduate school to earn a master's in secondary education.

In November 2009 came the life-changing call from Victor Hurtado. Meanwhile, Meredith's life was already about to change: that same month, she married her sweetheart of several years, Noel Campbell. The Melchers and the Campbells were neighbors, and the two met at a Christmas party in 2004. "We became friends then but not romantically involved yet," says Campbell. "That happened a couple of years later."

Campbell was already several years into his seven-year stint in the Army, first as an infantry officer with the 101st Airborne (Air Assault, aka the helicopter unit); later

Above: *Melcher aboard the U.S. Navy medical ship* Comfort.

with the Third Infantry Division, with which he served in Iraq for a year. Campbell tried civilian life upon his discharge in 2006, "but pretty soon the economy tanked, and my Army skills didn't seem that relevant in the job market," he says. Meanwhile, the defense contracting industry had been growing rapidly, so he decided to try his hand at contracting. Currently he serves as team leader on an "emergency reaction team" for the U.S. embassy in Kabul, whose responsibilities include physical deterrence, responding to potential crises, and ensuring convoy security for personnel traveling back and forth to the embassy, which, if you read the grim headlines about attacks on convoys in Kabul, translates from dry militarese into a highly dangerous job. As Campbell regularly

assures his family and others, working in the capital is much safer than other parts of Afghanistan, "even if every few weeks something goes *boom*."

He's a light-hearted soul, though, claiming that he and related Campbells— a grandfather who flew Navy fighters in Korea, his father piloting riverboats in the Mekong Delta, a brother in the Marine Corps—joined the military out of a desire for adventure more than anything else. "I was never one to keep things conservative and safe," Noel admits: he's still riding freestyle bikes and pursuing other extreme sports, even building himself a BMX ramp outside his compound in Afghanistan. He does get serious when mentioning that he hopes his job will enable him to build a nest egg for him and Meredith—to whom he proposed on Christmas in 2008, after they had carried on a mostly long-distance relationship for several years.

Naturally a huge fan of 4TROOPS, Campbell gets to watch some of their media appearances while in Afghanistan via the Armed Forces Network. To him, Meredith's music was "a nice bonus" amid her other accomplishments and gifts. "I know she harbored no illusions about how difficult a music career is. It was her fantasy pipe dream, and she was doing the sensible thing by going for her education degree."

Above: *Noel Campbell on horseback in June 2010 near the former site of the Olympic Pool in Kabul, used as the training facility for the national team until the Taliban banned swimming.*

So much for that, at least for now. "I never even thought this could happen," Melcher says. "Music has always been entwined in my life, and I consider singing almost critical to being able to function normally. It's such an outlet for emotion and communicating with others," she adds. "I just never thought I'd be singing professionally, so I'm still in shock," she says.

Victor Hurtado isn't so surprised. "She has that businesslike side, but don't be fooled. When Meredith opens her mouth, glory comes out," he says. "And sometimes a little bit of Aretha [Franklin]." Melcher loves the 4TROOPS repertoire and especially the way the arrangements are constructed to draw listeners into a narrative. "I think the fact that we trade off lines a lot makes each song more of a story. We do try to tell stories with the music—and with our different backgrounds and voice parts, and the way we sing." She especially enjoys the chance to portray, in different songs, "both the woman warrior and a woman at home. It's true to life, that's for sure—women are doing so much more in the military these days, on the front lines and taking more leadership roles."

> Music has always been entwined in my life. I consider singing almost critical to being able to function normally.

She believes deeply in 4TROOPS' mission of service to veterans, active-duty military and their families, and feels it's especially timely. "I worry sometimes that our people serving overseas aren't in the forefront of our minds anymore," she says. "There are probably fewer care packages now, fewer kids in schools sending messages. But there are still people doing very dangerous things over there, and it's important to keep that focus." In her thoughts, of course, is Noel Campbell in Kabul. Not only that: "My younger sister will deploy overseas in a year or so when she's done with the Soldier Show. And she'll probably be there longer than I was in Iraq; these days tours are twelve to fifteen months or more." Her own deployment was one thing, but it will be another thing to watch her "little baby sister" go to war.

Meanwhile, Melcher and her fellow group members will carry on with their mission of music to their once and future comrades. As she says, "You always hope to live your dream, but the reality is most people don't. I can honestly say that I'm living my dream, and I think that's what makes this so surreal." ★

Former Sergeant
Daniel Jens

"One time in Iraq I was playing my guitar out in the hall, and the next thing I knew almost my entire battery was surrounding me and having a good old time. It made me feel really good that I could do that. There's something about soldiers being at war that just takes things to a whole new level of closeness, so to be able to provide that service . . . it's just a nice break in a place like that. Kind of a light out of the darkness."

Growing up in Milwaukee, Wisconsin, Daniel Jens found rock 'n' roll dreams by watching Elvis and the Beatles on TV—and especially by hearing the adoring screams of their female fans. He was soon singing along with the radio "every chance I got," and friends started telling him that he sounded pretty good. From the very start, singing was a way for Daniel to get beyond whatever was painful in his life. The first big hurt came when his beloved father, Dennis Jens, died of a heart attack when Daniel was just five. It was a huge test of a little boy's faith: he prayed in vain for three days before learning that his father didn't make it.

His own biggest fan was his mom, Nancy Jens, who encouraged him when he picked up a guitar as a young teenager. "I think my musical gift probably came from my mom. She used to sing when she was younger—she never pursued it but she was always playing music in the house, everything from Motown to rock to country," Jens remembers. "I'd join in and she'd say, 'If that's what you want, go after that dream. Get as good as you can possibly be.' She was the one telling me to follow my dream, even later when everyone else was telling me to get a real job."

Not until Jens was nineteen did he have his own guitar. "Once I started to get a few chords down, I'd sometimes play for six or eight hours." Incorporating singing along with his playing was a challenge, but one day it just happened as he was figuring out the chords to the Guns N' Roses song "Patience." At twenty, Jens joined a rock band called Illegal Entry. "Our first gig was in a dive bar with no stage. As I sang the first song, no one was really paying attention, but when I got to the part when I could belt it out, every head turned at once and the rush I felt from the crowd was intoxicating. I was hooked."

He played in several other bands, the most successful of which toured around Wisconsin and other Midwest cities, and got a little airplay. He also worked at jobs in construction or sales to get by, but stubbornly hung on to the dream of a music career.

Though they didn't bring fame, his gigs with a group called One Less Infinity did lead Jens to the true light of his life. "It was at one of our Milwaukee shows in early 2003 where I first saw my future wife, Caroline," he recalls. "My pick-up line was, 'So, you wanna go make out in the band room?'" Instead, they went on their first date about a month later, on Valentine's Day, and married in December 2005. During those years, both also became involved in the Apostolic Life Church in Waukesha, Wisconsin. Singing in church, Daniel started to feel that his real values were out of sync with how he was living. "Trying to chase that rock 'n' roll dream and living the party lifestyle just wasn't doing me any good," he admits.

The sense of purpose he was seeking crystallized after the events of 9/11. Like so many others, he began to think about enlisting in the military and eventually did. The Army came to provide a solid support system for him and his family, even though they had to leave their familiar Milwaukee environs to settle in Fort Hood, Texas. When his number came up in October 2006, Private Jens deployed to Iraq for fifteen months with the 1st Cavalry Division (3rd Battalion, 82nd field artillery) as a cannon crew member. He drove a Paladin—a mechanized howitzer that fires artillery—and his detail was responsible for convoy escort, supply missions, and making sure VIPs moved safely through the country.

"I'd probably say the first month was a little scary," Jens says. "We caught small-arms fire. A rocket-propelled grenade flew over the trunk of my vehicle. Another time I had a rocket fly over my head and it landed thirty yards away. You've got mortars dropping. You're driving convoy missions and you've got bullets bouncing off your vehicle, IEDs exploding. You tend to get a little used to it after awhile."

During his deployment he sang at everything from prayer breakfasts (a common time to reflect and join in a communal meal) to talent nights at the U.S. Embassy. The music that meant the most to him, though, was singing informally for himself and his

mates, wherever they found themselves. "Even though I didn't have a guitar at first, I had buddies who would let me play theirs. Sometimes after a mission—it could be maybe thirty-six hours long—you're tired but still wound up, your adrenaline is flying high," he reminisces. "So I'd just sit and play. And it would help me wind down, put me in a place where I could feel 'I'm home now.' Or it would take me back to being at a campfire by the lake with my wife.

"I'd even forget I was in a war sometimes. Other soldiers would come around and ask 'Do you know this song?' Sometimes I did, other times it was like, 'No but I know this song.' And lots more people would gather around. Many times I'd be surrounded by my whole platoon or my whole battery."

One thing Jens never got used to was being away from Caroline and their kids: daughter Kayla, son Zech, and Caroline's son, Nick. The strong Christian faith he and Caroline shared helped them through the rough spots: they exchanged a series of email journals in which they explored personal issues with guidance from scripture. "It was a tool to

Opposite: *The young Daniel Jens with his mom, Nancy, in Bay View, Wisconsin.* Above: *Private First Class Jens in Baghdad, on the parade ground leading to one of the monumental Swords of Qādisīyah (Hands of Victory), triumphal arches built by Saddam Hussein.*

help us get through our task," Jens explains, "to get to the other side of my deployment with our marriage in one piece." Caroline Jens has even written a book about the experience, using those letters.

Music helped too. A song that had special meaning for him then, and even more now, was Jimmy Webb's "Galveston." Jens felt like he was living the lyrics, seeing the "cannon flashing" as he tracked artillery going downrange from his Paladin, and dreaming of his wife in Texas—Fort Hood, not Galveston, but close enough. When Webb later praised his rendering of the song on the 4TROOPS CD, Jens was "honored and speechless."

In January 2008, he came home from Iraq to a loving welcome. And his musical career was about to shift into high gear: that spring he tried out for the NBC-TV hit show *America's Got Talent*. His journey on the show started in April, when he auditioned in front of the judges in Dallas. After getting a standing ovation from the audience and enthusiastic feedback from the judges—Sharon Osbourne told him, "As soon as you started I got goose bumps"—Daniel advanced to the next round in Las Vegas. There he was chosen as one of the Top 40 to perform live in Los Angeles, and eventually made the Top 20. Ultimately Daniel placed eleventh in that season. The exposure seasoned him as a performer, and the attention he attracted was life-changing.

His debut on the show was performing Edwin McCain's song "I'll Be," and when he sang the tender lyric "I'll be the greatest fan of your life," he looked toward the wings where Caroline was watching proudly. The show's host brought her onstage for a joint

Above: *Jens and buddies pose by another Saddam Hussein monument in Baghdad.*

Sometimes after a mission you're tired but still wound up, your adrenaline is flying high. So I'd just sit and play. And it would help me wind down, put me a place where I could feel "I'm home now."

interview, to more cheers from the audience, and Daniel said, "This is what kept me going [in Iraq] . . . I'm so glad I could share this opportunity with my wife. It could be the beginning of a new life for us."

It proved to be the first key step was when *America's Got Talent* producer Nigel Caaro introduced him to Victor Hurtado of Army Entertainment, who immediately recognized a strong candidate for his roster of military performers and began sending Daniel out on gigs. That autumn, he performed at the Association of the U.S. Army's annual convention in Washington and at the 234th U.S. Army Birthday Ball in the nation's capital. With a friend, Sean Bennett (who had appeared on the show *Nashville Star*), he recorded a few songs, and Hurtado helped arrange for them to be heard on radio.

The Army fates also had a hand in giving Daniel lots of performing opportunities that year. Just after leaving *America's Got Talent*, he learned that his unit was being deployed again under the Army's "stop-loss" policy. Earlier, Jens says, he had been told that he would be transferred to III Corps, which meant that instead of staying in for another year—probably with another tour overseas—he would soon have been discharged. "But instead they transferred me to the Public Affairs Office of First Cav," he says. "So I actually got stop-lossed to stick around for another year on rear detachment, performing for the Army instead of going back to war." It was a blessing in disguise, he thinks, not only allowing him to stay at Fort Hood with an extra year to consider his future plans, "but my command gave me the freedom to get gigs and play on behalf of the Army."

Yet his good fortune also brought a dose of survivor's guilt, knowing that his buddies were going back to Iraq. A good friend he had served with was soon killed by a sniper; another member of his old battery had a sergeant die in his arms during a rescue. "I was starting to question what I was doing, just playing music while they were making the ultimate sacrifice," he recalls. A few things happened to change that. A memorial was held at Fort Hood for the fallen Sergeant Webster, and when Jens found out, he put in a request to perform. He sang another Edwin McCain song, "Prayer to St. Peter," which asks St. Peter to make sure heaven's gates are kept wide open for those who died serving their country.

"After the song, I got in the receiving line to give my condolences to the sergeant's

wife. Mrs. Webster took the trouble to say Sergeant Webster was proud of me for making it so far on *America's Got Talent,* and Mrs. Webster thanked me especially for coming to sing that day. I think that gave me a second wind to go on singing on behalf of soldiers, made me feel what I was doing was worthwhile."

In November 2008, Jens was invited to perform at another memorable event. The fervent letter of appreciation he later received from the lieutenant colonel in charge tells the story:

> SPC Daniel Jens provided an absolutely amazing series of musical and vocal performances during a new home dedication day for a Wounded Warrior in Oakland, Fla. The "Home At Last" Special Project was the first home built by Habitat for Humanity for a combat wounded veteran . . . SGT Joshua Cope, his wife, Erica, and their toddler daughter, Laney. SGT Cope was severely wounded

Above: *Jens, center, acknowledges applause after winning the first Black Jack Idol contest in 2007. Performers with the 2nd Brigade Combat Team, 1st Cavalry, sang weekly at the Black Jack Bistro dining facility at Forward Operating Base Prosperity, Baghdad.*

in an IED attack in Iraq in 2006 while serving with the 1st Infantry Division. . . . It was our distinct pleasure to witness SPC Jens perform at three separate events on Dedication Day. ... Jens [also] showed his versatility by playing some background music at the beginning and then a series of cover tunes at an encore performance near the end of the program. . . . It was awe-inspiring to witness SPC Jens, a combat veteran Warrior-Singer-Songwriter, honoring SGT Cope, a fellow warrior who gave both his legs in the defense of his beloved country.

Jens still feels humbled by the experience. "Even though I was officially being a blessing to them, it was a blessing for me to do it," he says. "That's when I really started to see what music could do—and that the Lord had blessed me with this talent for a reason."

Committed to the Army through January of 2010, Jens continued to do his job at Fort Hood while singing at every chance. But his *America's Got Talent* performances were attracting many eyes and ears on YouTube, including those of the DSW principals. And with their initial email inquiry to Daniel, 4TROOPS began to gestate. "I had two months left, and I was attending a class that helps you build your résumé for civilian life," Jens recalls. "That's exactly when the first message from Winston came in."

Key moments stand out for Daniel since the 4TROOPS train roared out of the station. One was during the pivotal showcase for Sony Music. He remembers that "as soon as we got done singing, Andrea Johnson [of the booking company The Agency Group] said, 'So when do we start booking this?' I think that's when I knew it was going to happen." He remembers the intense pressure of learning songs and arrangements for the recording, and then the special moment when he purchased his first copy in a New York store. "It's like all the hard work came to a head when I saw our CD on the shelf. I became very emotional and had to walk around the aisle, hiding my face until I could collect myself."

In January, Daniel and Caroline and the kids finally went home to Wisconsin, where Daniel hopes one day to have "a little place by a lake." They resumed attending their church in Waukesha, where he works with fellow musicians to organize and deliver weekly worship when he's not on the road, spreading the gospel through song. His music

It's like all the hard work came to a head when I saw our CD on the shelf. I became very emotional and had to walk around the aisle, hiding my face until I could collect myself.

ministry is as important to him as his work with 4TROOPS, and he hopes someday to develop an album that reflects contemporary Christian rock and worship yet can cross over into mainstream radio.

He loves keeping track of the public's response to 4TROOPS on their Facebook page. "We have received so much great support and wonderful comments from service members, their families, and civilians," he notes. "The touching stories of how our music is making a difference recharge our batteries and remind us of the important mission ahead."

He's been getting this kind of feedback for some time. One of the hundreds of comments on Jens' YouTube clips from *America's Got Talent* sums up the general reaction in a very few words: "Good job, soldier. Thanks for serving, thanks for singing. Nice thing for entire world." ★

Above: *Jens with his guitar, Killeen, Texas, March 2009.*

THANK YOU FOR SHOWING YOUR LOVE

SSG RON DEMETRIUS HENRY
OPERATION IRAQI FREEDOM
FEB 2003   CAMP MOSUL   FEB 2004

46

(see page 75). After winning the preliminary round at his home base of Fort Eustis, Ron went on to Fort Gordon, Georgia, as one of five finalists. There he delivered stellar performances and earned glowing comments from the judges. Some who followed the show claim he should have placed higher, or even won the competition.

Following his success on *Military Idol*, SSG Henry was tapped by the Command Sergeant Major C. C. Jenkins at Fort Eustis to join an established singing group of Transporters there. The group, known as "Transportation Express," was subsequently commissioned by the Installation Commander as a full-time entity with Henry at the helm. He became a Senior Enlisted Vocalist along with his regular Transporter job—which now meant being the road manager for the group. With nine vocal and instrumental performers, the Express went on to become one of the most successful singing groups in the Army, traveling to Alaska on assignment to lift the morale of families whose military parents were serving back-to-back deployments. "It was wonderful to see the appreciation in the eyes of those families," Ron says.

"We did a lot of performing on the base too," Ron recalls, "at parades, ceremonies, army balls, and 'safety shows'"—where soldiers going on leave get positive, awareness-raising messages about staying safe, especially on the roads at holiday time.

The ink was barely dry on Ron's discharge papers when he was tapped to be the fourth member of 4TROOPS. Says Victor Hurtado, who had inaugurated *Military Idol*, "After seeing Ron's amazing talent there, I kept in touch and brought him in to do one-time shows now and then. He had such a desire and will to improve as an artist; he was always asking me, 'What can I do better?' There's a real humility and respect for those he trusts." When Hurtado and the DSW team were looking for that key fourth member of the group, "I didn't even know Ron was out of the Army yet," admits Hurtado. "I was on a train from D.C. to New York when I heard, and the first thing I did was call him."

Ron now lives with his wife, Tabitha ("the queen of my soul"), not far from Fort Eustis in Hampton, Virginia, where he worships and sings with the Tower of Deliverance Fellowship church. It's close enough that, when 4TROOPS performed at the base in early

Opposite: Henry times three in a souvenir poster from Camp Arifjan, Iraq. Above: Ron plays electric piano at a gospel concert at Camp Arifjan.

May of 2010, he could commute to work. "It was fun to have my wife, my church family, and lots of my Transporter buddies be able to come to the shows."

Henry's drive to learn and improve would serve him well during his hectic initiation with the group. One reason Hurtado thought he'd be right was his range—"he's got that nice low tone but he can go high as well, and their repertoire has lots of intricate harmonies where the voices have to switch between high and low."

Fitting into those harmonies was one of many hurdles Ron faced in his new fellowship. "I came into the group a little later than the others, and at first it was very challenging for me, because all my life I'd been used to singing lead," he notes. "I knew how to sing background vocals but hardly ever did it. So I had that mindset that I always wanted to be the leader—but I knew this was much more about teamwork." He would work with Hurtado, at first, then with music director David Lai, learning how to control his volume and his breathing so he could fold smoothly into the beautiful blend that is a hallmark of 4TROOPS. "They'd show me how to tell if I was too loud, how to bring it up a little here or down a little on another note. Learning to do that was so fulfilling," he says. "Like being birthed again in music."

> I had that mindset that I always wanted to be the leader—but I knew this was much more about teamwork.

Above: *Ron with his Transporter buddies and Iraqi soldiers they had trained, in an Iraqi guard compound, Mosul, Iraq, August 2003.*

Another challenge for Henry was the repertoire chosen for him, especially the song "Dance with My Father," on which he sings lead. He found it daunting for both professional and personal reasons. "In the first place, of course, this was sung by the late Luther Vandross, an outstanding vocalist in the R&B realm, and here I am, a new artist just coming up and trying to do it justice," he says. "And then it was personal for me because I grew up without a father. So the lyrics were hard to relate to at first: the story of a boy with a father in his life, but who then passes away. Emotionally that was hard, and also to be reminded of my own loss or lack. Even in rehearsals and during the recording, I'd have tears in my eyes when I sang it." But the song makes him grateful, he says, "that I did have men in my life who gave me direction."

He's also grateful to have been exposed to such a wide range of music while growing up, in church and elsewhere, believing that has helped him connect with 4TROOPS and with material he's less familiar with, such as country stylings. "Even at the community chapel services, you had to be flexible. You'd have a gospel service and then a Protestant service, and the music didn't always mix. You had to be sensitive to what people wanted to hear in their worship; it wasn't always hand-clapping and shouting. I'd have to ask, how can I reach these people without shoving what I know into their ears? You can't be closed off musically to just your own ideas."

Ron appreciates that with 4TROOPS, "we get to do a lot of things: a little country, rock 'n' roll, some inspirational or traditional or contemporary songs, even a little Broadway." But it's the spirit behind the repertoire that keeps him going. "We sing together like we're family. We act like we're family. It's in line with the Army motto: We take care of our own," Henry explains. "That's what we've been doing together since we came together. We take care of one another."

> I feel like God has entrusted the four of us with something special.

Wherever 4TROOPS goes, Ron can be found reaching out to audiences as a joyful and irresistible ambassador. He can barely believe in what's happened over the last few months: "I'm forty-one years old and retired from the Army, and if you told me two or three years ago that I would be sitting right here, I would be just like: 'Y'all crazy.'" But he does firmly believe that all of it "has been divinely done by God."

Especially the opportunity to bring music to his former fellow soldiers and their families. Another song with special meaning (and a lead vocal) for Ron is "Here We've Been," penned by Victor Hurtado as a testament to the steadfast courage of those who serve in

combat. "It's about how you don't back down from what you have to do," says Ron. "We were scared in Iraq, but we knew what we had to do, and we did it.

"All my life I've prayed and asked God to lead me in a path where I can be a light for others," he says, "and that's why I have to believe that I didn't just accidentally fall into this opportunity with the other troops. I feel like God has entrusted the four of us with something special: that we can give back to America now, help people out who are depending on us, and assist the veterans organizations as well. So whatever I have to do—every song, every autograph, every handshake—I'll do it. Because you never know how your actions are going to affect someone, like my grandmother told me. It's truly an answered prayer." ★

Above: *Ron shared some love with members of the cast of the 2010 U.S. Army Soldier Show when 4TROOPS traveled back to Fort Belvoir, Virginia, to mentor the young performers in April 2010.*

Former Sergeant
David Clemo

"Being in the military was good training for what we're doing now," David Clemo believes. "We're used to coming a long way in a short time. You do preparations, you get training, but there was never a time in the military when a real-world situation was just like what you'd prepared for."

Although he "never imagined" what he and 4TROOPS are doing these days, in a sense Clemo has been preparing for this experience his whole life. Both his grandfathers served in the military, and his father, Michael Clemo, was a surveyor and forward observer in the Army Artillery during Operation Desert Storm. Born in Fort Carson, Colorado, David's early years were spent on the road: the family moved to Germany, Oklahoma, and Georgia before finally settling in Mount Vernon, Washington. He fondly remembers working at his grandparents' tulip farm in the Skagit Valley, and he still favors a quiet rural lifestyle—a far cry from his current life with 4TROOPS.

Clemo focused on sports early in his childhood, but his prodigious musical talent soon showed forth. "In my early teens, I started playing guitar and singing with my uncle in church," he reports. "Then in high school I joined the jazz choir," where he first got a taste of the tight harmonies that 4TROOPS specializes in and where his beautiful high tenor was much prized. He also did some local musical theater, playing Danny Zuko in *Grease*, the young Scrooge in *A Christmas Carol*, and other parts. When he went on to Skagit Valley Community College, he again sang in the jazz choir.

For us, being soldiers just makes it easier to adapt to what's happening now.

"I got lots of compliments and pretty much got my head swelled," he says. "People were urging me to move to Los Angeles, and I started to believe I really could make it as a performer." So he went south and gave it a try but fell prey to the classic small-town-kid-in-the-big-city syndrome. "I got into some problems," he admits, "mostly economic ones. I wanted to get my act together, and the military seemed like the best way to do that."

He signed up without telling his family first. And when his mother, Maria Kerley, found out he had elected to join the Army's Airborne Corps, "she was very surprised. I was her only son, and she just said, 'Are you sure?'" His dad would have talked him out of it, reminding him that being in Airborne usually meant a rapid deployment overseas. In the end, they accepted his choice, "though they felt like they'd worked to give me a different path," Clemo says.

But Clemo, who feels most at ease when he knows his assigned role in an organization, adapted to Army life without a hitch. His father was right about one thing: he was going away soon. His "reception" date was September 6, 2001. And his official military ID bore the date it was issued: September 11. Clemo did his Airborne training from September 2001 through June 2002, and that November left from Fort Bragg, North Carolina, for Afghanistan with the 50th Signal Battalion, 35th Signal Brigade (in support of the 18th Airborne Corps).

Clemo's job was to provide communications support for major logistics and fire bases. But he didn't necessarily end up doing exactly what he had trained for. Typically, he notes, "I would be thrust into a situation and had to adapt. For example, my job was supposed to be setting up phone lines." But when he got to Afghanistan, the circumstances often called for jobs with unfamiliar equipment. "So at ten o'clock at night, someone would say, as a training exercise, 'OK, Clemo, get out there and do the job.' And I'd figure it out somehow—read manuals, go talk to people, get some codes. You just use what you learn in training to help adjust to the situation you're in."

> I wanted to get my act together, and the military seemed like the best way to do that.

Music took a back seat for the first months of Clemo's Army career. "When I was in basic, guys would request songs and people would join in if I sang something, just a cappella." When he began active duty with the Airborne, he had plenty to do just learning the job and getting his feet wet. Once in Afghanistan, though, he hooked up with a friend who had an acoustic guitar and a digital recorder, and they did a lot of playing and singing together. "The guys that ran the computer network had a database with music and TV shows we could access," he recalls. "And they would also upload a few of our songs to the database, so other soldiers could hear them."

Shortly after his first deployment, Clemo made an interesting discovery: through his guitarist friend Jonathan Walker, he learned that the Army fielded a touring show of singing troops. "The way he explained it, I thought it was like joining a band," Clemo says. "Anyway, we sent in a tape." In November 2003, they auditioned together and both were accepted into U.S. Army Soldier Show.

"It wasn't until then that I learned the show involved a lot of movement—choreographed dancing. It's a good thing I was more nimble in those days!"

Clemo thrived on the taxing grind of life in the Soldier Show—rehearsing, performing, setting up and striking sets, doing public relations, and lots of travel. It was in the Soldier Show that Clemo first recognized how powerfully his music could affect other troops and their loved ones. During one of the meet-and-greets after a show at an American base, a woman in the audience requested to address the cast. "A family member of hers had recently passed," Clemo says, "and she thanked us all personally for lifting her up. She said it started the healing for her." When you've lost someone close, he believes, you tend to close down, "but music is something that can touch you and allow you to talk about it, let the healing process begin."

His year-long tour went by quickly, and in its final month, he learned that he was facing another deployment. Within a week of the tour's end, in November 2004, he was on his way to Iraq, to serve for the next year as a chief of a team that installed fiber optic cables on the base. Since he was known as a singer by his new command, Clemo again was asked to appear in talent shows,

Above: *David Clemo, right, played Danny Zuko in a community-theater production of* Grease *while in high school.*

chaplain services, and national anthem gigs. "If you have any type of singing ability, you become kind of a hot commodity," he says.

While performing with the Soldier Show, he had formed a strong bond with Victor Hurtado, at that time Artistic Director of Army Entertainment and the show's director. Hurtado noted in his voluminous mental files that young David Clemo was not only a preternaturally gifted singer but had a good head for organization and an unflappable temperament. So he waited for the chance, and when Clemo's Iraq tour was over, brought him back to the Soldier Show as an assistant director. In 2005, Clemo embarked on the most fulfilling three years of his life, helping to develop the talents of his fellow soldiers and maintain the integrity of the touring show. "David has wonderful performing instincts and was so generous about sharing his gifts and experience with the new casts each season," says Hurtado.

Clemo's new job came with a significant bonus. In the cast of the 2008 show was a petite blonde from upstate New York, Specialist Joann Usyk—a parachute rigger in the 623rd Quartermaster Company, 18th Airborne Corps, based at Fort Bragg, North Carolina. Army regulations precluded a backstage romance but they became great friends. After they were discharged (his came in October 2008), David and Joann's relationship blossomed and they soon began making plans for a life together. Those plans took on an-

Above: *Sergeant Clemo with an Afghani man.*

Letter to McKenna

While touring with 4TROOPS in the spring of 2010, David Clemo wrote a letter in installments to his daughter in the womb, who was born on June 21.

March 6

I was trying to think of ways to give you an idea of how I am feeling while you are in your mother's belly. I figured this would be the most real and raw way to do it since I'm going through it right now. When your mother came down the stairs that day and told me she was pregnant I was very excited and very scared. We were both trying to finish school and get a life started together after the military. You were definitely a surprise but never thought of as a mistake.

. . . If I'm still singing for a career when you are reading this, it was the single most difficult decision I ever made because it meant that I had to spend time away from your mother and you. We took the chance because not only was it a noble project but also it could possibly give you the life that I feel you deserve.

The second ultrasound of you was the next single most amazing day of my life up to that point. I saw your spine, brain, arms, legs, and your heart. Seeing it beat at 140 beats per minute blew me away. I wanted to tell you that I love you right then and there.

. . . There isn't a moment that goes by that I'm not thinking about meeting you for the first time. When you find out you are going to be a dad, you don't really know if you are ready since you can barely take care of yourself. It's scary and exciting and I want to make sure that I don't mess up.

March 10

Well, it's another day and I'm sitting in a hotel room away from you and your mother. It doesn't look like it will ease up for a bit either. I struggle with wanting to go home and doing this for a job. My mom tells me that I should see this through but I feel like you and your mother suffer the most through all of this.

. . . I know we are going to disagree and fight sometimes. We might not understand each other, but the day I found out that I was going to be a father I had this feeling inside that I was to protect you from all the bad things in life. It doesn't mean that I don't think you can't handle it. I just think it's hard to watch your child go out into the world and have to fight the whole world off. No matter what, you will always be my little girl.

. . . It's funny how when I was growing up my parents would say these things to me and I never really knew what they meant. Now I understand what it means to love someone unconditionally. I do love you more than life itself and I will do everything I can to make your life better than what I had. If I don't have you and your mother in my life I have nothing. —Dad

other dimension when Joann became pregnant in the fall of 2009—"at almost exactly the same time we found out about the 4TROOPS project," says Clemo, still amazed.

Since these two major developments in his life, Clemo's heart has been in two places at once: with Joann and their daughter (born June 21, 2010) and onstage with his comrades in 4TROOPS, wherever they find themselves. "I would love to continue in music and I couldn't be more proud to be singing with this group," he says. "The only conflict I have is that I'm really excited to be a dad. Ever since I found out we had a child coming, it's all I can think about." While on the road, Clemo intermittently wrote an extended letter to his unborn daughter (excerpted in the accompanying sidebar).

For now he's at peace with his commitment to 4TROOPS and their upcoming tour, and copes cheerfully with life as a touring musical artist. "When I performed in and directed the Soldier Show, the pace I had to work at definitely prepared me for what's happening now," Clemo says. "As a soldier, especially on deployment, you're used to being in a high-stress environment, living on deadlines and having people tell you what to do."

He views 4TROOPS' style of music-making as a true expression of teamwork. "The way we share songs with each other, trading off on the lead, really reflects how things are in the military. Our lives were like that: not all just singing harmony or one person always in the lead, but sharing both roles."

Even their repertoire reflects what he remembers about singing in the Army. "The songs about saying goodbye, and about staying motivated so you get back alive, really ring true," he says.

"I think music is the most powerful force there is to make people feel something. That's why I think we were given the gift of music," he reflects. That very power of music can make 4TROOPS' mission an emotional balancing act at times. "The hardest part about singing to a military crowd," he feels, "is seeing emotion rise up in the audience—sometimes you can tell that a person out there has lost a loved one, or maybe they've been seriously injured or suffer from PTSD. It's hard to look them in the eye and keep your own composure, not let it affect your singing.

"But mostly I'm ecstatic because it's great to be able to give back to people who laid the groundwork for us. The way we're being treated now is because of what the guys in Vietnam went through, what the guys who were in Korea went through, what the guys who were in World War II went through . . . So I'm completely honored to be part of helping veterans make the transition back to civilian life.★

> The songs about saying goodbye, and about staying motivated so you get back alive, really ring true.

Boot Camp

The provisional 4TROOPS, together with their mentor Victor Hurtado, convened in New York City in early December of 2009. Some were meeting each other for the first time; for others it was their first visit to the Big Apple. And the pressure was on big-time, because in just under three days, they were slated to audition for Sony Music's MASTERWORKS label—an event that would determine if they had a future as a musical group.

Sony MASTERWORKS had been instrumental in the project from the start, independently exploring the idea of an act that would somehow connect with the military, and talking with the principals at DSW Entertainment about how to make it happen. As MASTERWORKS General Manager Alex Miller puts it, "We wanted to find a project that could do well, as well as doing good."

Miller had strong personal motivations for wanting to do something on behalf of veterans, tracing back to his response as a New Yorker to 9/11. "I found it very disturbing," he says, "to see veterans begging or homeless on the city's streets at the same time as we were seeing members of the military out there protecting us—at airports, or coming off the train at Penn Station." In contrast to the gratitude expressed to the soldiers protecting New York, it seemed like the nation rewarded some of those former servicemen and women by saying, "You're on your own."

Also in early December 2009, Miller notes, President Obama was about to announce that more troops were headed to Afghanistan in a renewed push to make progress in that long conflict—which in turn would produce more veterans with unmet needs.

"So with this as the backdrop, the question became, how can music help?" he recalls. The discussion between Sony Music and DSW began there and led eventually to the all-important tryout on December 7. Meanwhile, the soon-to-be 4TROOPS and Hurtado found themselves in a Manhattan rehearsal studio with just a piano, keyboard player David Cook, and four microphones. They also had a handful of songs that DSW and Hurtado had identified in recent weeks and for which Hurtado had worked out simple arrangements. He handed out assignments: this singer would be featured on this song; you're on this harmony line, you're on that one.

"We worked up five songs for the showcase, with harmonies and arrangements," says Hurtado. They began with "For Freedom" (which would become the group's first single), and also performed "Here's to the Heroes," "You Raise Me Up," "You'll Never Walk Alone" (the perennial anthem of hope from the Rodgers and Hammerstein musical *Carousel*), and Irving Berlin's "God Bless America."

Meredith Melcher was encouraged by what she heard, even this early. "It didn't take long for me to start noticing the others' strengths, what each individual brought to the table." Recalls Daniel Jens, "We had just a couple of days to work up four or five songs, so we worked pretty hard." And David Clemo characteristically points out that "the military was good training because there you're used to coming a long way in a short time. This was similar. You just have to not let the stress affect your focus."

Those around the 4TROOPS remarked—not for the last time—on their unflappability. But for them, Winston Simone observes, coolness under fire isn't just an abstraction. "When you've had people firing rocket launchers around you, it sets a high threshold for nerves."

And then the day came. "We were waiting on a fire escape outside the DSW conference room, so we could kind of make an entrance," Jens remembers. Crowded into the room were upward of twenty-five executives and staff from Sony Music and The Agency Group (booking agents), along with the DSW team.

"The door of this dimly lit conference room opened on a bright shaft of light, and in walked four smiling enthusiastic young people," says Alex Miller. "They didn't say anything, just starting singing." After "For Freedom," they went right on to a second song and the remaining three without a break, accompanied only on keyboard. When they finished, says Miller, "there was a big round of applause, a standing ovation," something very unusual for a music audition.

Mindful that the group not only had to sing but also to articulate their mission to the public, Miller started asking questions. Did they know what they were doing, and why? Did they really have the desire to follow through with this? "I asked them each to intro-

Each of the members of 4TROOPS was quite different in voice and personality, so you don't want to lose that—each should be able to shine.

—DAVID LAI, MUSIC DIRECTOR

duce themselves and explain why they were here. And I was so deeply affected by the stories they told, and by their humility."

"'I'm David Clemo,'" one of them said, 'I was born on an army base, and my father and grandfather served.' And he described his mission in the war." Each talked about how proud they were of their service, about their dreams of singing, and about how they'd come to realize that returning veterans have important needs that are often frustrated. "And they felt that a mission could be accomplished by embodying those needs as a group, using music to get their message across.

"None of it was scripted," Miller adds. "All our fantasies that we might be able to find people like this were realized, with no prodding or artifice. We came out saying 'wow' over and over.

"So they not only passed the audition in terms of musicality, but in the other way that was so important: that they be strong representatives of all veterans," he adds. "They

Above: 4TROOPS at Downtown Studios with, left to right: Jennifer Liebeskind and Laura Kszan of Sony MASTERWORKS, makeup artist Monica McAlpin, Winston Simone of DSW and his son Winston, Victor Hurtado, and Dexter Robison, also of DSW.

could be the perfect messengers for a mission of service, and fulfill their personal desires to have a career in music."

The 4TROOPS project was now put on a fast track, aiming toward the launch of a debut CD to be released around Memorial Day the next year. All the machinery of bringing a new musical act to the public was set in motion: the recording deal itself, decisions about repertoire and genre, who would produce the CD and how to record it, cranking up the publicity and marketing apparatus, even working out the group's onstage look.

Above all, though, was the task of shaping the group itself, from a collection of part-time singers whose performing experience had been mostly in the Army, into a polished,

professional unit that could record and perform at the high level everyone was aiming for. For this they needed help beyond what Victor Hurtado, busy with his full-time Army job, could provide. Next to join the 4TROOPS team was David Lai, a protean whirlwind of a musician who not only served as a Senior Vice President of A&R for Sony MASTERWORKS, but in his spare time conducts on Broadway (currently *The Phantom of the Opera*), and is a Grammy Award–winning record producer.

"At first I was coming in from the A&R side to manage the project," says Lai. "But because things had to move so fast, I ended up working closely with the group as a musical director and coach." It was immediately clear to Lai that these were four very talented individuals who didn't yet know each other musically, or how to use their gifts to greatest effect. "So the focus of my energies was to help the four of them become one group, working on all the aspects crucial to creating a great sound via harmonic blend, rhythmic precision, uniform diction . . . everything important to ensemble singing—to make the most of what each of them brings to the mix."

The pressure was on again, because the group was already booked to tape an interview and performance for *Good Morning America* on December 18. "The repertoire was already in place," Lai notes, so he could concentrate on the group's vocalism.

"You always want to figure out the strengths of an artist and develop those. Each member was quite different in voice and personality, so you don't want to lose that—each should be able to shine. Yet they all need to be at the same level when singing together:

Above: *Music director David Lai, left, and Victor Hurtado.* Opposite: *4TROOPS in rehearsal with David Lai.*

keeping the breathing, intonation, phrasing, and especially keeping the emotional focus consistent." Lai notes that they all could read music, "but this was more about the ability to be musical, to use their ears, and get to that level playing field."

Like everyone who has worked with them, he was impressed by their dedication and discipline. Those were qualities Melcher, Clemo, Jens, and Henry would need to draw on constantly in the months to come: in interview after interview, in rehearsing for and recording their CD, and in live performances at venues ranging from Major League Baseball parks to a NASCAR racetrack to the deck of the aircraft carrier *Intrepid*. As 2009 drew to a close, all this still lay ahead—and the group remained unfazed, if a little dazed.

"To be honest, I'm surprised every day," says David Clemo. "I'm a very simple person; I grew up working on the farm from age thirteen, so for me this type of lifestyle—what we're doing, how fast it's happening, the people we're meeting—I never imagined I'd be here."

In their quick ascent, 4TROOPS have inspired everyone who crosses their path. As music director David Lai puts it, "When I met them, it really struck home what the sacrifice is that soldiers make. It's one thing to read about it in the media, but when you become close to people, like these guys, it's suddenly very real. It's like having your first child—you don't know what love is before that. And it makes me deeply appreciate what 4TROOPS are doing." ★

Entertainment for the Soldier, by the Soldier

"A lot of people don't imagine that troops can sing or dance or act," says Former Cpt. Meredith Melcher. "I think they would be surprised to know that the military has many programs directed toward promoting the talent of troops—which is a really good outlet for soldiers who are creative."

The members of 4TROOPS come from widely differing backgrounds and native locales. What they all share, of course, are their talent and passion for singing and performing. They are also linked by their histories with the Army Entertainment Division, which is—as people may also be surprised to learn—the largest producer of live entertainment in the world today.

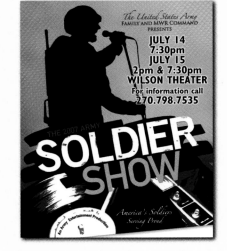

Since getting its start in World War I, Army Entertainment has operated under the motto: "Entertainment for the Soldier, by the Soldier." It's hard to imagine someone who better incarnates that principle than Victor Hurtado, the AED impresario who brought the members of the 4TROOPS together. "These four are not only a testament to the wealth of programs provided by the Army," says Hurtado, "but they also reflect the skills of those professionals who have developed them as military leaders and as artists." As one of those professionals himself, Hurtado, now in his 25th year in the Army entertainment business, should know.

The son of Mexican immigrants, Hurtado began his musical career at age nine as a member of the Compton Boys Choir. In 1986 he joined the Army, where he served as a Communications Security Specialist with the 2nd Armored Division. After being discovered singing in the shower at Fort Hood, he toured for four years as a solo artist and with the U.S Army Sol-

Opposite: *Soldiers sing Myron Butler's "Stronger" while marching in battle gear during the 2008 U.S. Army Soldier Show.* Above: *Poster for the 2007 Soldier Show.*

dier Show, where he also served as Assistant Musical Director, while continuing to serve in his artillery unit. As a sergeant, Victor began to follow in Irving Berlin's footsteps by creating arrangements and writing music for his fellow soldiers. He left the Army in 1990 and moved back to his native California to pursue his music career but in 2001 was asked to rejoin the Entertainment Division to direct the Soldier Show. He held the post of Artistic Director of Army Entertainment until 2008, and since then has been developing military talent and partnering with service-member entities on many fronts, while still serving as Production Director of the current Soldier Show.

These days the Entertainment Division is part of an umbrella entity known as FMWRC: the Family and Morale, Welfare and Recreation Command of the U.S. Army. Based in Alexandria, Virginia, FMWRC attends to soldiers' well-being in the broadest sense by offering programs for travel, sports, outdoor recreation, the arts, and of course entertainment. Its professionally staffed and highly organized entertainment units have come a long way from the earliest origins of soldier entertainment during the American Revolution and the Civil War.

Back then, Army camp shows were often spontaneously organized in companies, battalions, or other units with volunteer soldier entertainers. The Civil War gave rise to many military songs that are still well known, sung then by soldiers from both the Union and Confederate sides—sometimes in earshot of each other. The division's historian has unearthed many such details—for instance, while stationed near Fredericksburg, Virginia, the Battalion of Washington Artillery of New Orleans performed a farce called *Pocahontas, or Ye Gentle Savage* with Confederate General James Longstreet in attendance.

In 1918, Sergeant Irving Berlin's *Yip! Yip! Yaphank* officially began the tradition of entertainment for soldiers by soldiers as the first incarnation of the Army Soldier Show (see sidebar "Sound Off!" page 70). Berlin's show and George M. Cohan's song "Over There" provided rallying and rousing patriotic music for soldiers and civilians alike, as troop entertainment became an essential morale booster during World War I.

Between the wars, Special Services programs (as they were then called) suffered from underfunding, but World War II brought a renewed commitment to lifting the morale of troops in all the theaters of war. Draftees provided the talent and inspiration for the 1942 Broadway soldier show *This Is the Army,* which Berlin wrote, directed, and produced. The show's cast and crew were members of U.S Army Special Services Company No. 1, which also became the first integrated World War II company in the armed forces. Wartime focused Berlin's energies like nothing else. "Songs make history and history makes

Opposite: *Pfc. Daren Taylor (center) is flanked by Pfc. Kevin Waul Allen [left]*
and Spc. James Becton (right) during the 2004 U.S. Army Soldier Show at
Fort Belvoir's Wallace Theater. Above: *A production number from the 2007 Soldier Show.*

Sound Off!

The Irving Berlin Center, headquarters of the U.S. Army's Entertainment Division at Fort Belvoir, Virginia, is named in honor of the Army's most famous musical veteran. In 1917, the iconic composer of more than 1,500 songs was drafted, prompting newspapers to trumpet "Army Takes Berlin!" Posted to Camp Upton, in Yaphank (Long Island), New York, Berlin was asked by the Special Services (then so called) to create entertainment for the troops serving overseas in World War I.

At Camp Upton, Berlin—an insomniac used to keeping show-business hours—found himself lying awake at night "listening to the strange sounds that came from the other cots," he wrote later. "I have no idea what time I fell asleep, but I woke up with a start and heard for the first time the bugler who was to become my pet aversion." That bugle call inspired "Oh, How I Hate to Get Up in the Morning," and that song was the basis for Berlin's musical revue *Yip! Yip! Yaphank!*, which opened at Camp Upton's theater in 1918, moving on to Broadway that July.

Cast mainly with Army recruits, including men dressed as Ziegfeld girls, it featured a mélange of songs, dancers, and acrobatics, plus military drills choreographed to music by Berlin. Besides the big number, its songs included "You Can't Stay Up on Bevo," "Kitchen Police," and "Mandy" (later used in Berlin's score for the military-themed movie *White Christmas*). One tune Berlin wrote was scrapped as too downbeat for the occasion; in 1939 he resurrected the tune and wrote new lyrics for the most popular patriotic anthem ever: "God Bless America."

During the finale, "We're On Our Way to France," the whole company in full gear would march down the aisles and out of the theater. One night in September, at the end of the run, the finale got a new twist when Sgt. Irving Berlin and the whole crew joined the cast marching out into the street—most of them headed to France for real.

When the United States entered World War II, Irving Berlin came back to Camp Upton to do firsthand research for a new show, *This Is the Army*, which opened at the Broadway Theatre on July 4, 1942. A huge hit, it toured the U.S., European combat zones, and the Pacific theater, and in 1943 became a movie starring George Murphy, Joan Leslie, and then–Lt. Ronald Reagan. Berlin donated all his royalties to war charities: for this generosity and for his singular contributions to lifting home-front morale, he received the Medal of Merit from General George C. Marshall. ★

Left: *Irving Berlin performs aboard the USS Arkansas in 1944.* Opposite: *Sheet music cover for "Oh! How I Hate to Get Up in the Morning."*

songs," he said. "It needed a French Revolution to make a 'Marseillaise' and the bombardment of Fort McHenry to give voice to "The Star-Spangled Banner.'"

As the war went on, celebrity draftees like Mickey Rooney entertained troops in stateside training camps, staging areas, and overseas units. Soldier "Jeep Shows" and Special Service Company Shows took live entertainment to combat areas. The Entertainment Section prepared scripts for musical revues in booklets titled *Soldier Shows Blueprint Specials—By the Men . . . for the Men in the Service.*

The need for organized soldier entertainment eventually led to the hiring of Civilian Actress Technicians, or CATs. As a woman's professional publication reported in 1946, "It was found that the American soldier likes his 'theatre' two ways: the traveling USO camp show and the soldier show that he stages for himself." The CAT program was conceived as a way to use the resources of female entertainers while so many men were at war, and starting in 1945, these women served in the Pacific and European theaters to organize, direct, perform in, and present musical, variety and theater productions by and for soldiers. More than a few well-known actresses of the mid-20th century, including Florence Stanley and Pat Carroll, spent time as CATs.

In the 1950s, entertainment platoons of the 10th Special Services Company lightened the spirits of troops in Korea. Beginning in 1966, civilian women again took a major role in supporting troop morale with the Army Special Services Program in Vietnam. They coordinated USO tours; produced, directed, and acted in theater productions at larger base camps; and developed Command Military Touring Shows, composed of in-country military personnel who entertained their fellow soldiers in areas where commercial shows could not go for security reasons. In the 1970s, programs for the children of servicepeople were added, as the Music and Theater program continued to expand and adapt to meet the needs of the changing Army.

> Songs make history and history makes songs. . . . The bombardment of Fort McHenry [gave] voice to "The Star-Spangled Banner."
>
> —IRVING BERLIN

Today, Army community theaters alone stage more than 900 productions annually worldwide for audiences totaling a quarter of a million. Soldiers carry on the tradition of music "for the soldier, by the soldier" through several current programs. The U.S. Army Concert Tour is a summer concert series that brings top-name artists to military families and their communities. (Toby Keith was the featured artist in the May 29 show that opened the 2010 series.) The

USA Express, AED's deployable musical performance group, is a highly energetic, six-to seven-person, Top 40-variety show group composed of active-duty, National Guard/ Reserve musicians and singers. Geared musically for younger soldiers, USA Express tours to remote installations, training sites, and isolated combat contingency areas.

The Army has sponsored several different musical competitions in the last decade or so. Victor Hurtado was largely responsible for conceiving and creating the current contest *Operation Rising Star*, originally known as *Military Idol*, based on the hit show *American Idol*. (See sidebar on page 75 for details.)

But the most ambitious and far-reaching of AED's programs is the annual U.S. Army Soldier Show, reconfigured in 1983 as a high-energy, ninety-minute ensemble musical review. Staged entirely by active-duty soldiers who travel more than 25,000 miles to perform for audiences totaling 100,000-plus, the song-and-dance extravaganza offers a wide range of popular music and stage spectacle to troops and families on Army garrisons worldwide. The performers, chosen by Army-wide audition each year, are amateur artists with a passion for performing who come from supply, medical and emergency, animal care, transportation and aviation, legal and law enforcement and other tactical units. They must be recommended by their commanders and have outstanding military

Above: *Mickey Rooney (second from right) and members of his USO show feed troops chow, October 12, 1952.*

records, as well as demonstrate musicality, movement, stage presence, and versatility. (The dance audition sometimes proves the most daunting, as it was for 4TROOPS' David Clemo.) The show also recruits audio and lighting technicians based on their military and civilian theater experience, recommendations, and military record.

The show is assembled in five weeks and then tours for six months. Once named to the cast, soldiers are attached to FMWRC for the duration of the tour. Soldiers in the cast and crew are expected to adhere to standards of military physical fitness, deport-

ment and appearance. They are assigned specific military responsibilities and show duties commensurate with their rank, in addition to their functions and responsibilities within the show, such as vocal director, dance captain, wardrobe/costume manager, technical crew chief, and stage manager.

The new cast and technical crew spend six weeks at the Entertainment Training Center in Fort Belvoir, rehearsing under the direction of the artistic staff. Twelve- to sixteen-hour days begin with a military formation and include aerobic workouts, vocal coaching, dance training, and learning how to assemble and dismantle the stage trusses. The technical crew learns computer-based lighting and audio and video functions while designing the lighting, sound, and special effects. Besides learning choreography, performers memorize as many as 40 songs, including country, R&B, gospel, rock, oldies, soul, and patriotic songs combined in solos, duets, groups, and fast-paced production numbers.

Once on the road, soldiers work an average fourteen-hour day, seven days a week for seven months. At each stop on the tour, the cast and crew offload, load, assemble, and dismantle eighteen tons of equipment including four miles of cable and one hundred theatrical lights. During the tour, they handle more than a million pounds of electrical, sound, stage and lighting gear for the totally self-contained show. Some soldiers have described it as their toughest duty outside of combat. The Soldier Show is funded not with taxpayer dollars, but with funds generated from business programs of MWR and with generous corporate sponsorship.

Above: *During the 2008* Operation Rising Star *competition at the Wallace Theater on Fort Belvoir, left to right: Co-host Victor Hurtado, host GeNienne Samuels, winner Joyce Dodson, and runner-up Fatima McElveen.*

Operation Rising Star

Military Idol—launched in 2005 and re-named *Operation Rising Star* in 2007—was the brainchild of Coleen Amstein, who worked for the U.S. Army Community and Family Support Center, and Victor Hurtado, then artistic director for the Soldier Show. "I had been working with the *[American Idol]* production team for a while, and in the back of my mind I had wondered how we could put something together for our soldiers," says Hurtado. Amstein had been thinking along similar lines, and when they connected, Hurtado contacted FremantleMedia, which holds the rights to *American Idol*. Getting permission to use the "Idol" name was a great asset in jump-starting the program.

Troops with singing talent at bases around the world answered the call. One was Staff Sergeant Ron D. Henry, a Transporter based at Fort Eustis—though he almost missed out. "A friend of mine found out about it on the very last day you could apply," Ron recalls. "She'd heard me sing and insisted I go sign up, even called the MWR director and begged them to let me in."

In the inaugural 2005 competition, first-round auditions were held at thirty-six Army installations in the U.S. and overseas. Contestants had to be vocalists—no dancing or comedy routines—and perform a cappella in these preliminaries. In the *Idol* mold, a trio of judges (including military brass and local celebrities) narrowed the field, then spectators voted to choose who would advance from each base. Ron Henry won the Fort Eustis contest, earning a $500 prize and a trip to Fort Gordon, Georgia, to compete in the finals, to be broadcast as a live, ninety-minute telecast on the Pentagon Channel. "I couldn't get over how much talent the Army had represented there," he marvels. "We all shared stories about how we got into music, sang on the bus, and got close over those few weeks."

Henry made it into the top five, and treasures the compliments he got from judges Michael Peterson, the country artist, and songwriter Mark Wills, whose song "Back at One" Henry coincidentally chose for his last performance. The winner that year was Sgt. William Glenn, a forty-two-year-old National Guardsman based in Darmstadt, Germany. Reflecting a truly Army-wide contest, *Operation Rising Star* has been staged at bases throughout the U.S., in Alaska and Hawaii, Germany, Japan, Korea, and even Iraq.

"These folks represent the Army in a positive way with something that's exceptional," says Hurtado. Ron Henry, the soldier who wowed Hurtado in the 2005 competition, has gone on to bigger things with 4TROOPS, but to him it's all part of the same endeavor. "My hope through all of this is that we continue to touch the lives of Americans, of armed forces, of people across the world." ★

Meredith Melcher and David Clemo of 4TROOPS both performed in the cast of the 2004 Soldier Show, and Clemo later served as an assistant director under Hurtado for three years. Ron Henry was a top five finalist in *Operation Rising Star* as well as leading a musical group of fellow Transporters at Fort Eustis. Daniel Jens spent his last year or so of Army service singing and playing his guitar at a variety of military events, often arranged by Victor Hurtado. Each member of 4TROOPS points to their Army experiences and training as a driving force behind the group. The training they received equipped them to perform on the next level, they say, and soldiering through deployments in Iraq and Afghanistan helped prepare them for the adversities of touring and recording.

"Never in my wildest dreams did I ever think that the Soldier Show, let alone my time in the Army, would ever lead to something like this," declares Melcher. But the connection is clear to her. "All the skills I now take with me as a recording artist are about building relationships and being responsible for your actions, which the Army taught me. Being on time at the studio, being respectful of other people's time and experience and energy—really not taking anything for granted and just being mindful and appreciative of the whole process."

Ron Henry agrees wholeheartedly. "Discipline," he explains. "Being respectful of others; not burning bridges; just trying to create peace and harmony no matter what situ-

Above: *David Clemo (in red shirt) performing in the 2004 Soldier Show.*

ation you're in. I want to show the world that we are a team—whether Army, Navy, Air Force, Marines, Coast Guard, we all serve a purpose and we couldn't do without one or the other. We all need each other.

"The most important thing is I want to stay humble and grateful for where I am," Henry adds, "and the Army Entertainment Division had a whole bunch to do with that."

"If I hadn't joined the military and been involved with Army Entertainment, I wouldn't have learned both sides of performing, and I definitely would not be here," says David Clemo. "It gives me a better appreciation for what I'm doing now. The skills I learned there have made this so much easier for me."

4TROOPS has found at least one way to say thank you to Army Entertainment. In late March, the group returned to the Wallace Theater at Fort Belvoir to meet and offer encouragement to the 2010 Soldier Show cast.

"These guys are phenomenal," reports Ron Henry. "The coordination, the harmony, the dynamics, the excitement in their voices, it is just mind-boggling. So much energy and so much joy in what they were doing. This is true Army talent from all across the world. I'm so emotional within my heart to see what's still coming behind us and what we paved the way for."

Henry got a big surprise at this mentoring reunion. Soldier Show performer Spc. Demetria Stewart has a daughter to whom he is godfather, but neither Henry nor Stewart knew the other was involved with the show. "This sweetheart right here, we go back like four flats on a Cadillac," Henry told the group. "I've known her since 2000. I had no idea she was here."

Stewart did a double-take when Henry entered the theater. "I had no idea that he was in 4TROOPS and he did not know that I was in the show."

> The skills I now take with me as a recording artist are about building relationships and being responsible for your actions, which the Army taught me.
>
> —MEREDITH MELCHER

For Meredith Melcher it was also a family reunion, though she knew in advance that she would see her younger sister Katie, a current cast member. "That was really cool to see the next generation of troop talent," she says. "To share our music with them and have them share some of their music with us is just a really cool experience. And the fact that my sister is in the show makes it more special for me. When I see her in the Army Entertainment sweats, it just brings back a lot of memories."

Melcher, Clemo, Henry, and Jens sang for the cast and huddled with them to share

their incredible experiences with 4TROOPS. Demetria Stewart sums up the impact: "They gave us some inspiration," she says. "They gave us advice of what to look for and what not to do, and it also gave us motivation to see where we could be in the near future. We're starting now and we're developing, so this is like a foundation."

Victor Hurtado made clear to his young cast what the 4TROOPS have done to open doors for soldier-performers. "They're carrying the weight now of the new genre of military music, and you guys are coming up," he told them. "[Because of them] you're going to be far more visible." Hurtado loves that 4TROOPS took the time to mentor the next generation, and saw its effect right away. "One of the troops in the new show said to me, 'If we ever thought that you weren't going to take care of us once we leave, the proof is here.'

His fondest hope is that other performers coming out of the military may break out in similar style. "This feels like a pavement project for future troops," he comments. "It feels like it's paving the way because it's solid and it's real and it's good. Hopefully, we'll have other veterans and troop artists following in their footsteps." ★

Above: 4TROOPS, seated, watch the cast of the 2010 Soldier Show singing "We're Going to Make It," written by the cast about resilience.

Raised my hand, raised my weapon
Now I raise my voice
For the brave, those who served
I will carry the torch . . .

To defend, to stand tall
Through the fire, through it all
Always ready, we've stood by your side

—Lyrics from "Here We've Been,"
Victor Hurtado and David Ylvisaker

Part 2

MARCHING ORDERS

Hello, America!

For its first two months of existence, 4TROOPS was a stealth group. As they began working on their sound, recalibrating their lives, and in some cases separating from the Army, their support team was coalescing around them and laying plans: for their first media and public appearances, their first big concert, their first recording, and their first tour. Photo shoots were staged; promotional videos were shot. Studio time was booked, arrangements written out, luggage purchased.

But as 2010 dawned, the group also rose up on the horizon. A red-letter day was January 26, when Sony MASTERWORKS announced the signing of the group in a major press release, with the news quickly picked up by *Billboard*. That same day *USA Today* ran a story on the group headlined "Band of Brothers-in-Arms," which led appropriately with, "Somewhere Irving Berlin is turning red, white and blue."

And that morning, America was introduced to 4TROOPS over the airwaves, as

Melcher, Jens, Clemo, and Henry were interviewed and performed their signature song "For Freedom" on ABC's *Good Morning America*. Announcing the segment, which was titled "Healing with Music," anchor Robin Roberts said, "Now, from the battlefield to the recording studio, the story of four veterans who are just back from Iraq and Afghanistan. They . . . immediately set their sights on a different mission—music. Bob Woodruff joined them for a recording session."

That would be Bob Woodruff, the ABC correspondent and news anchor who in January 2006 was severely wounded in Iraq by a roadside

Opposite, top: 4TROOPS perform during the first live TV performance on Good Morning America. *Opposite, bottom: 4TROOPS with Robin Roberts and George Stephanopoulos. Above: At a Fox local station.*

bomb while embedded with the U.S. 4th Infantry Division. Since his recovery, Woodruff had been very active on behalf of injured veterans through the Bob Woodruff Foundation and ReMIND.org, which provide resources and support to service members, veterans, and their families—especially around issues of reintegrating post-service—and raise awareness of their needs. So it was no surprise that as soon as Woodruff heard about 4TROOPS and their parallel mission, he arranged to interview them. In fact, though it aired in late January, the interview took place in December, just a few weeks after the showcase audition and only days after Ron Henry joined the group.

The group met with David Lai and Woodruff at Manhattan Recording Studios in Times Square, the home away from home for producer Frank Filipetti, where they were practicing some early arrangements for their CD. They sang a cappella, and Woodruff was so inspired by their music and stories that he sat down at the piano to accompany them in an impromptu rendition of "Lean on Me"—afterwards joking with Roberts about how badly he played.

But the encounter took a sober turn when Woodruff asked the former soldiers about their service. Describing her work in the early days of Operation Iraqi Freedom, Meredith Melcher said, "We made it all the way up through Baghdad to Balad and established the first troop medical clinic there. We evacuated hundreds of American and Iraqi casualties."

Woodruff looked stunned. Clearly this hadn't been part of his briefing. "You helped set up the hospital in Balad?" he blurted. "The place where my life was saved?" Later, in voiceover, he adds, "It was there, almost exactly four years ago, where ABC cameraman Doug Vogt and I were treated and sent on the road to recovery after being hit by an improvised explosive device. Without soldiers like Meredith, I would not be here today."

As Sony MASTERWORKS' Alex Miller observes, "You couldn't have scripted that. And it was just one of many amazing moments of synchronicity."

Each member of 4TROOPS spoke thoughtfully about their experiences and their hopes for what they can accomplish as a group, setting a pattern for countless interviews

Above: 4TROOPS performing for the Walmart conference in Orlando. Opposite: 4TROOPS at Fort Hood with cyclists about to embark on the Ride 2 Recovery, which raises funds to help injured veterans overcome obstacles.

to come. Dan Jens noted, "Really, it's bigger than us as a group. It's not about us making it, but that we're standing in a gap between veterans, soldiers that are deployed, and the families of those soldiers." Victor Hurtado filled in some background on how 4TROOPS formed, saying, "I knew them as solo artists, but I also knew that coming together they would become a lot stronger. We're forming a unit, if you will."

After *Good Morning America*, they were off and running. February brought appearances on *Fox & Friends* (the first of several) and a slew of reports in military publications: *Army Times*, *On Patrol*, *Military Wire*, and the Army's Entertainment Division website.

In early March they ventured out to perform live at a Walmart managers' conference in Orlando, and at a full-blown concert on board the *Intrepid*, filmed for a PBS special. They performed the National Anthem before thousands of spectators at NASCAR's Food City 500 Sprint Cup race in Bristol, Tennessee. Says songwriter Marcus Hummon, whose "Bless the Broken Road" is on the 4TROOPS CD and who played with them at a performance, "I was nervous for them—it's a tough audience. But they won everyone over with their passion."

Once recording sessions for the CD wrapped up, 4TROOPS hit the road for a flying tour of U.S. military bases, from Andrews Air Force Base in Maryland, to Fort Sam Houston and Fort Hood in Texas, to Fort Eustis in Norfolk, Virginia. Every live gig, every in-studio performance or interview, was another step in transforming a collection of recent vets and sometime singers into an assured, professional musical act. Those around them still marvel at how much they seemed to take in stride.

"They did things that even for seasoned people would be extraordinary," says Winston Simone of the DSW team. Alex Miller raves about the "absolute bravery" the group members displayed on this new front: "This is a very competitive business. They'd been together something like ninety days, had learned songs, gone into the studio, completed a recording, sung live on TV and in front of a huge NASCAR crowd . . . it's remarkable." Bob Woodruff was struck by the 4TROOPS telling him that "the battlefield had prepared them well for the tough music industry."

"I can't think of anything in my years in the music business that's been more organic in how it's come together and the way it's been embraced," Miller adds. "No one has said no. Any opportunities for media to spread the word, or for citizens to meet 4TROOPS, have grown into still more opportunities." ★

Live from the *Intrepid*

Backlit, they stride through smoke and haze, past the aging machinery of a ship of war and onto a stage set up in front of the vintage airplanes inside the hangars of the *Intrepid*. Cut to a drummer in parade dress making his way through the audience as he beats out a solemn cadence. The audience, a tapestry of civilians, veterans, active-duty troops, and their families, sits on metal benches, leaning forward in anticipation. It's March 15, and 4TROOPS are about to kick off the first big public concert of material from their forthcoming CD. Not only that: the show is being filmed for broadcast on PBS stations across the country—and for release on DVD.

Behind the performers, a large projection screen flashes images of events from *Intrepid*'s storied past. As they walk to their mics, we hear the piano intro to "For Freedom" and a soldier selected from the audience just moments before announces in foot-drill tones, *"Presenting . . . 4TROOPS!"* David Clemo raises his mic and begins, "Somewhere a trumpet sounds in the night / A soldier is standing there. . . ." Daniel Jens picks up the line, then Ron Henry, then Meredith Melcher, and the voices meet in harmony. As the song unfolds, they move around the stage naturally, changing positions, making contact with each other and the audience, trading off lines in solo, duet, and quartet. Photos from their lives and Army careers come and go on the screen, along with other military imagery, ending on a rippling flag as they sing ". . . and for freedom she'll ever wave!"

4TROOPS
Live TV Special

Please join us and 4TROOPS for their PBS special at the U.S.S. Intrepid

March 15th, 2010
Seating at 6:30 pm
Show begins promptly at 7:00 pm
Pier 86, W. 46th St. and 12th Ave.
New York, NY 10036

When they finish, the crowd erupts in cheers, and the joy and relief on the group members' faces is plain to see. Those are predictable emotions for performers putting on their first big show and getting a great reception to the opening number. The relief has another source as well. The production truck had arrived hours late, delayed by a storm that had flipped cars and closed highways up and down the East Coast. Then a tiny technical glitch held up and finally derailed the dress rehearsal.

Right: *Invitation to 4TROOPS' live performance and filming on board the* Intrepid.

"By the time we traced three wires randomly patched, the audience was coming in," says Shelley Ross, who produced and directed the show and the sixty-minute film. Producing a live concert from a truck on land cabled to a ship floating in the water had some built-in challenges. "You have to be careful—because the tide is always going to be at a different level than when you cabled up." Once the "mystery glitch" was solved, Ross had to direct a live show with a crew of ninety, most of whom had never heard or seen the group before. "I was the only one who knew what was going to happen."

Ross is a veteran producer who won three Emmy awards and the distinguished Peabody Award for her work at ABC News, where she was executive producer of *Good Morning America* and *Primetime Live,* clocking more than 2,500 hours of live TV. She is married to DSW founder David Simoné. Ross was already brimming with ideas for the concert film. "It was perfect for PBS: the appeal would be national and multigenerational. And since it's not a broadcast network, it could be presented in the PBS concert format," keeping the focus on 4TROOPS and their audience.

"My first task was to come up with the right venue to provide a visual backdrop for the concert. " Ross scouted West Point and contacted various military bases before settling on the aircraft carrier *Intrepid,* a vessel steeped in military history. As soon as she toured it, she knew this was the only place to introduce 4TROOPS.

"Once I heard 4TROOPS' personal stories, I didn't just want to produce a concert with pretty songs and pretty lighting. My challenge was how to bring the deeper meaning of the songs to the small screen. So I created a story arc for the show that, in my head and heart, is like a veterans' pop opera. First we invoke the spirits of the *Intrepid.* Then we start introducing themes—for example, the first set of songs speaks to family, freedom, and mercy or compassion."

Ross aimed to capture the spirit of the ship by making it part of the set. "What strikes you on the *Intrepid*, and looking at the photos of it in service, is the history that's embodied in every old stairway, all the coats of paint, every exposed pipe, every gnarly metal artifact. I wanted to light every bit, draw attention to it. In the very first song, 'For Freedom,' you'll see archival films and photos of the *Intrepid* being hit by ka-

What strikes you on the *Intrepid* is the history that's embodied in every old stairway, all the coats of paint, every exposed pipe, every gnarly metal artifact.—SHELLEY ROSS, DIRECTOR-PRODUCER

mikazes and burning at sea, the ghostly images of navy pilots who served and all those sailors who were buried at sea." 4TROOPS would be able to bridge that history and the generation now serving.

After "For Freedom," David Clemo introduces himself and then the group. With that, Ross notes, they start to seed their biographical details, "establishing their authentic humility and why they yearn to honor other veterans."

The next song is "Bless the Broken Road," a love song Clemo here interpreted for all military families that endure separation. Says Ross, "When he sings about wanting back 'the time I lost with you,' we see home movies of David and his father tossing around a football, and the family at dinner."

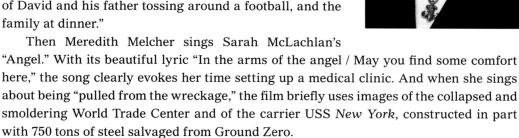

Then Meredith Melcher sings Sarah McLachlan's "Angel." With its beautiful lyric "In the arms of the angel / May you find some comfort here," the song clearly evokes her time setting up a medical clinic. And when she sings about being "pulled from the wreckage," the film briefly uses images of the collapsed and smoldering World Trade Center and of the carrier USS *New York*, constructed in part with 750 tons of steel salvaged from Ground Zero.

The theme of overcoming separation returns in the song "I'm Already There." Written by the lead singer of Lonestar to bridge the distance between him and his children while he was on the road, it was quickly adopted by many military families—including one first documented by Ross in 2002 and tracked down again in March 2010. The touching scenes of little girls singing the song while waiting for their dad to come home are from the Litchfield family's home movies of his 2002 deployment to the Gulf region. And 4TROOPS puts a new spin on the song by having Melcher musically portray a woman soldier far from home, while Clemo responds as the stay-at-home spouse and parent.

And so the songs unfold onstage and on film, each introducing a new musical side of the group, a new solo voice, a new story. In the second set, we hear about the brotherhood of arms, about the pain of loss and soldiers' fears of dying, about the joys and challenges of homecoming. "You Raise Me Up" becomes a paean to the singular bonds forged among troops serving under fire. The Vietnam era is evoked in the Jimmy Webb song "Galveston," a big hit from that era, stunningly interpreted by Dan Jens with his guitar.

Above: *Producer Shelley Ross.*

Introducing himself, Jens talks about the song as the rear screen shows images of him serving in Iraq, guitar slung on his back like a rifle. "I literally lived the lyrics for fifteen months in Iraq, "he says. "From simple things like cleaning my weapon to sitting in the driver's hatch in my Paladin watching artillery go downrange with the 1st Cav division, there were so many times this song brought me back home to my wife in Texas."

Now it's Ron's turn in the spotlight. First he leads the group and spectators in a rousing call-and-response cadence written for the occasion. Next the group launches into their version of Toby Keith's classic "Courtesy of the Red, White, and Blue," the show's most upbeat and overtly patriotic number. It brings down the house. But then Ron tells the crowd, "We're going to tone it down a little"—a prelude to his achingly beautiful performance of Luther Vandross' "Dance with My Father." The song follows two story lines of the pain of deployment. As Ron sings the lyrics, we see a Marine dad packing his duffle bag and lifting his seven-year-old daughter, Janessa, for a goodbye hug that may be her

last. We see her counting the days apart with a jar of M&M's labeled "Daddy comes home," and asleep at night holding a doll crafted from a photo of her dad.

In mid-song, the camera cuts away from Ron to follow Meredith as she walks out from backstage (now re-costumed in a Nicole Miller dress and army style shirt, both in military hues) and into the arms of her father, who we will soon learn is Lt. Gen. (Ret.) David Melcher. (See the sidebar on the next page.) As Ron sings, "How I'd love, love, love / To dance with my father again," the two circle slowly in the aisle, trading affectionate grins. Ron finishes the song with tears in his eyes, "because he knows what that yearning is, what that pain of separation feels like," says Ross.

The last set opens on a somber note as Dave Clemo says, "A friend of mine was killed in action in Pakistan a couple of weeks ago." He dedicates this group of songs "to his memory, and to all the fallen, and to those left behind." Dan Jens begins singing "You'll Never Walk Alone," and the others join as the Broadway anthem builds to its first chorus. On the repeated verse, it picks up a backbeat and a gospel tinge, as a choir led by

The General's Daughters

eredith's got a pretty good head on her shoulders. She was never the starving artist type waiting for her big break, so what happened with 4TROOPS was a bit of a surprise for her at first. But now that the ball is rolling, she's 100 percent committed. That's her way."

This could be any proud dad talking about his daughter's breakout career in music—but not exactly. This is three-star Lieutenant General (Ret.) David F. Melcher ("Call me Dave"), who with his wife, Marla, raised two daughters who became officers in the U.S. Army. Millions have by now seen him on the PBS special *4TROOPS: Live from the Intrepid*, dancing with his older daughter, Former Captain Meredith Melcher. They probably don't know that the youngest Melcher, twenty-four-year-old Katie, is a West Point graduate and a first lieutenant, currently following in her big sister's footsteps by performing in the U.S. Army Soldier Show.

The Melchers had mixed feelings about their daughters choosing careers in the Army, but Dave

Melcher wasn't totally surprised. "We had talked about it as Meredith grew up, and it would have been hard for her not to be influenced by all the soldiers around." That was true especially during his stint at West Point. While Meredith eventually chose a broader college experience at the College of William & Mary, Katie, who was born at West Point, "was bound and determined to go there, and did," graduating with her lieutenant's commission in 2008.

The Melcher girls may get their singing chops from Dave, who loves music and played trumpet in his younger days. Retired from the Army in 2008, he now serves as president of Defense and Information Solutions for ITT Corporation, managing its portfolio of businesses serving the defense and aerospace markets.

When asked to dance with his daughter during the song "Dance with My Father" in the *Intrepid* concert, the retired general's main worry was whether his uniform would still fit. That settled, he accepted. "She's a great young woman, and if I could do something to help her and the group, I was happy to do it."

Hugely proud of both daughters and their decision to serve, Melcher did worry when Meredith was in Iraq, but says that it was toughest on Marla. "I was in the Army for thirty-two years and gone a lot—in the field or deployed. So my wife deserves an awful lot of the credit for raising two wonderful young women. When a soldier is gone a year or more, it's those who stay home that keep families together."

Left: Meredith, left, and Katie Melcher pin on their father's third stars, October 2004, at West Point.

music director David Lai appears behind 4TROOPS. An Army choir had been enlisted, but someone belatedly discovered a rule that forbade their involvement on a commercially released DVD. So David Lai quickly reached out to the Broadway Inspirational Voices, a brilliant gospel ensemble comprised of some of the finest actors performing on and off Broadway. They learned and rehearsed the music for a couple of hours on the day of the *Intrepid* concert. Christopher Gattelli quickly joined in to create and teach them choreography for the concert.

This final act of the "opera" touches on themes of redemption, patriotism, and finally celebration. Continuing in the spiritual vein, a bagpiper intones the first strains of "Amazing Grace" as images of flag-draped coffins and fields of crosses are screened. Then Dan Jens offers a last word from the group: "Again, we are 4TROOPS, and we hope y'all are 'for troops' as well!" This kicks off a brisk closing medley of patriotic tunes: "You're a Grand Old Flag" segueing into "America the Beautiful."

> A friend of mine was killed in action in Pakistan a couple of weeks ago. . . . We'd like to dedicate this next group of songs to his memory.
>
> —David Clemo

As the performers leave the stage, the audience erupts into a standing ovation. So of course they oblige with an encore: it's the Kiss rock tune "Raise Your Glasses," now sung as a salute to all who serve.

Ross is proud that, despite the technical goblins, her production, with nine cameras shooting video, captured all the shots they needed to make a great film. She had sat through a week of studio rehearsals, "so I knew to put cameras one beat ahead of the move—like when Meredith puts her hand on Ron's shoulder." She also credits top Canadian producers Pierre and François Lamoureux and her "brilliant" editor Guy "Pico" Picotte, who shared her sensibility about how to balance performing shots with the background videos.

Most of all Ross credits the group for their talent, courage, and faith. "They trusted us," she says. Which wasn't easy without a dress rehearsal. "But I kept reminding them that it's not live TV," says Ross. "We could stop and restart if necessary; the audience would stay with them. But it wasn't necessary in the end, and I have to credit their fantastic performing instincts." ★

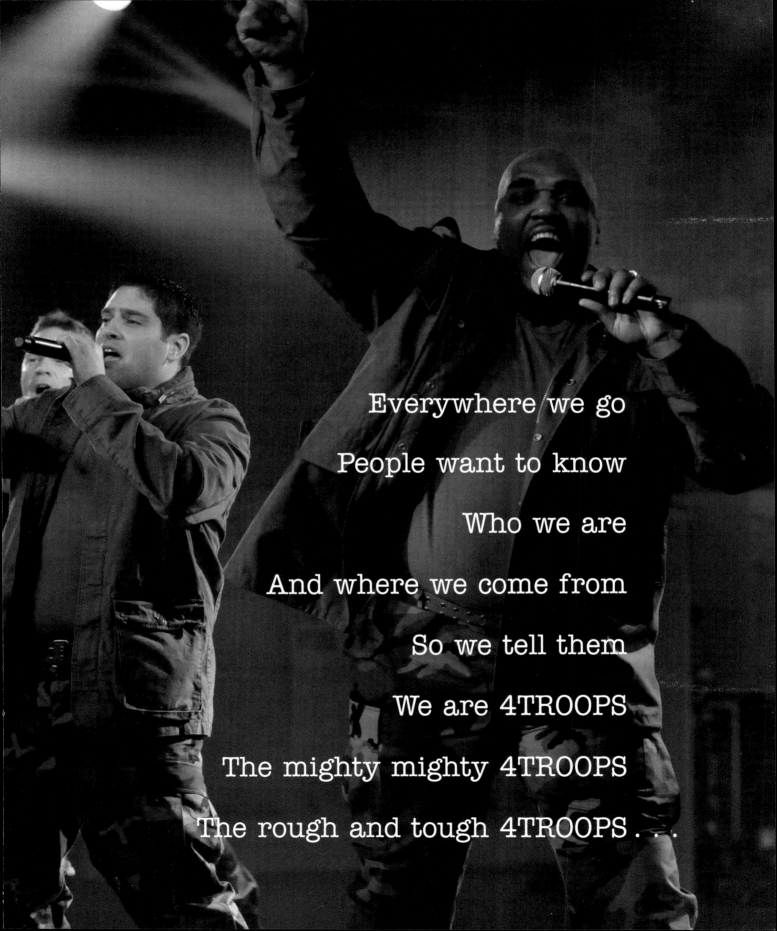

Everywhere we go

People want to know

Who we are

And where we come from

So we tell them

We are 4TROOPS

The mighty mighty 4TROOPS

The rough and tough 4TROOPS . . .

Home Team

Their TV appearances and concert film brought 4TROOPS into millions of living rooms, but there's nothing like live gigs to stoke excitement about a group. In the spring, Americans by the thousands assemble for the annual rituals of outdoor professional sports, and what better way to bring a taste of 4TROOPS to a sympathetic audience? By the middle of 2010, the group had performed at a NASCAR event, a stop on the PGA Tour, and at four Major League Baseball games.

"When you're seeking audiences, you ask: who would care?" says Winston Simone of DSW. "Baseball in particular has been disposed to honoring veterans—for example, the owners of the Mets have made veterans' groups their major charity."

4TROOPS' first exposure in front of a stadium crowd came on March 21 at NASCAR's most popular Sprint Cup race: the Food City 500 at Bristol Motor Speedway in Tennessee. They sang "For Freedom" as a pre-race song, standing on the finish line, with the drivers and their families watching appreciatively from the sidelines. They also performed the National Anthem; country star and NASCAR favorite Lee Greenwood sang afterward. They got a big hand from the typically restless crowd, and a fan wrote (in an Amazon review of the CD): "I first heard 4TROOPS before a NASCAR race at Bristol . . . and when they started to perform, they stopped me in my tracks."

On May 5, the PGA Tour presented a "Salute to Military Families" during the Players Cup Championship at the TPC Sawgrass course on Florida's Atlantic coast (where active, retired, and reserve members of the military can play for free). The 2010 Military Appreciation Day featured a Blue Angels flyover and 4TROOPS singing the

Opposite: *4TROOPS with a pace car at Bristol Motor Speedway.* Above: *Country star Lee Greenwood talks to the group before they perform.*

National Anthem. Ron Henry and Meredith Melcher, both golf fans, didn't get a chance to try out the course on this short visit but hope to return. "We don't get out to play as often as we'd like these days," says Melcher a little ruefully.

It was baseball that really stepped up to the plate to showcase 4TROOPS. On April 5, the group helped the Mets mark their home opener at CitiField ballpark on a day of great spectacle and ceremony. "Here to honor America with the singing of the National Anthem," intoned the Mets PA announcer, "please welcome four U.S. combat veterans of Iraq and Afghanistan. Ladies and gentlemen . . . 4TROOPS!" Melcher remembers the experience as "exhilarating" and Dan Jens says, "It was surreal . . . you're out there in front of not just all the fans but all the players from both teams too."

Not quite a week later, they sang for the Mets' rival the Philadelphia Phillies at their home opener at Citizens Bank Park. All agreed it was just as thrilling, with the Phillies coming off their 2009 World Series appearance and aiming for another great season. "It was phenomenal," says Henry. "The fans were really excited coming out the gate after last season, and the applause was just so grand and loud." Melcher caught the excitement and became a Phillies fan, at least for the day. "I bought the cap!"

The members of 4TROOPS are all baseball fans to some degree, with Jens probably leading the way in devotion to his Milwaukee Brewers—the team of his childhood. "I remember the last time they were in the World Series, back in '82, that team with Robin Yount, Paul Molitor, Cecil Cooper—all those greats. Now we've got a new ballpark, Miller Park, and it's just incredible. When that retractable roof opens up on to a bright sunny day, there's nothing better."

Clemo and Henry are both Atlanta Braves fans—Clemo liked the great teams of the '90s with their ace pitching staffs, and Henry grew up in Georgia. As for Melcher, "We moved around so much when I was a kid that I never really established roots with one team, so I ended up rooting for whoever was nearby. I live in the D.C. area now, so it's 'Go, Nats!' Wherever I am, I'll be a fan."

Above: *Ron Henry hawks programs at the Phillies Opening Day game.* Opposite: *4TROOPS on the Jumbotron at Citizens Bank Park (and, on overleaf, at Yankee Stadium).*

YANKEE STADIUM

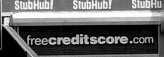

The 4TROOPS shared their thoughts on life and baseball in a series of interviews with an MLB.com reporter Tara Gore and recorded "God Bless America" at the MLB.com studios—all those clips viewable online. They were even asked to choose their "walk-up" songs—the snatches of music played for batters coming to the plate. Showing their rocker sides, Clemo chose Led Zeppelin's "Kashmir" and Jens took "Thunderstruck" by AC/DC. ("Back in the Army I used to use it as a marching cadence!") Melcher heard Justin Timberlake's "Summer Love" at the Mets game and it stuck in her head. And Henry would want "We Are the Champions," the perennial sports favorite by Queen. "And I could sing it myself!"

Another classic rivalry runs through the group's following two MLB appearances. On May 7, they sang at Fenway Park for a Red Sox–Yankees game, savoring the deep traditions of that venerable stadium and the passion of Red Sox Nation. But they had to admit that nothing could top their experience later that month in the Bronx. On Memorial Day, May 31, they performed the anthem at the new Yankee Stadium before the home team's game vs. the Cleveland Indians, and sang "God Bless America," a seventh-inning-stretch tradition since 9/11. Covering the game for *The New York Times*, sportswriter Joe LaPointe said of their National Anthem performance, "They wore camouflage and sang beautifully, a stirring interpretation of a song not always easy to sing."

Jens describes a baseball fan's fantasy day: "They treated us like royalty. We took pictures on the field, and during batting practice we stood us in front of the Yankees dugout and got our baseballs autographed by Derek Jeter, CC Sabathia, Mariano Rivera, Joba Chamberlain, Jorge Posada, and manager Joe Girardi. We even shared a luxury suite with Kelsey Grammer. Talk about a boy's dream come true!" ★

Opposite: *4TROOPS show off their baseballs autographed by Yankee stars.*
Above: *With Kelsey Grammer at Yankee Stadium.*

4TROOPS on Record

Releasing a 4TROOPS debut CD topped the list of goals for the fledgling group. An ambitious target date of May 2010—just before Memorial Day—was chosen, and the recording work became the constant background to all the group's activities in the first quarter of that year.

Choosing songs for the CD was a critical process, as those decisions would shape the group's identity. It began as a conversation among the DSW management team, Victor Hurtado, and Sony MASTERWORKS. Virtually soon as he began recruiting the group, Hurtado began to receive material from DSW to consider, and they traded lots of MP3 files. "It was a real collaborative process," Hurtado recalls.

Unlike a group that brings a well-established musical identity and repertoire to a recording deal, the field was wide open. A song's chief qualification was that it should fit 4TROOPS' mission of reaching listeners with a heartfelt message about the power of the human spirit, as embodied by our veterans and those in military service. Songs didn't have to be "about" military life in a literal sense, because that life embraces so many bedrock themes: family, separation and reunion, brotherhood, and love of home.

Nor did they have to belong to any particular genre or style. "As we were selecting songs, that issue did come up," says MASTERWORKS' Alex Miller. "We were looking at country, spiritual, pop, and outright patriotic songs." The 4TROOPS brain trust had a perspective unlike that of a typical recording company, where the accepted wisdom is that an artist must stick to one genre: you're a country act, or you're a gospel act. But feedback from the group and other research suggested that genre identity wasn't a big

Above: *4TROOPS CD cover.*

factor for young people in the military, or young listeners in general anymore. "Kids who grew up on country are singing hip-hop; soldiers who grew up in urban environments are getting into country," Miller notes. "What matters more is the camaraderie of getting together around music and the solace that brings. Those trump any individual taste."

It was also important, notes Winston Simone, that each song felt good to the group members. Because certain songs would showcase individual voices, "you have to imagine, can he or she sing this? The lyrics had to fit, because casting a song is sort of like an actor being cast in a part." Also, says Simone, "We didn't want it to get too rah-rah; we wanted the songs to tell stories that were upbeat and inspiring without being maudlin."

This approach suited the singers fine. They were vocalists with wide-ranging tastes and musical backgrounds, open to any song that spoke deeply to them. More than ever, Ron Henry appreciated having been exposed to all kinds of music in his youth, in church and elsewhere. "People would tell me to learn a Frank Sinatra album, learn a Benny Goodman album; listen to all kinds of different artists, how they attract their audience and what you could take from them. So I tried to take all that and put it with what I love to do."

> ## Here were four people with incredible solo voices. What they needed to work on was singing as a unit.
>
> —FRANK FILIPETTI, PRODUCER

Even so, assembling the ideal selection was a huge puzzle; by the time work had to start, they had settled on only seven songs out of the fifteen that ultimately were recorded. And choosing repertoire was just one piece of the puzzle. How would the songs be arranged, and how would the voices be assigned in each? What should be the overall sound direction, and what musicians would play behind the singers? How would the recording be planned and carried out? And how would the group learn the art and science of singing on a record, in record time?

Enter the cavalry, in the form of producer and sound engineer Frank Filipetti, an acclaimed industry veteran who had recorded and mixed albums for (among others) Carly Simon, Barbra Streisand, Vanessa Williams, George Michael, and James Taylor, including Taylor's Grammy Award-winning *Hourglass* in 1998. He had also recorded live albums, including the Pavarotti and Friends series, *Minnelli on Minnelli,* James Taylor's *Live at the Beacon,* and Elton John's *One Night Only,* as well as original cast albums for *A Funny Thing Happened on the Way to the Forum, Annie Get Your Gun,* the Tony Award winner *Aida,* and the Grammy Award winners *Wicked* and *Spamalot.* Talk about time pressure: as Alex Miller notes, "When you produce a Broadway show, you have to

do the entire recording in one day—it's intense beyond imagination." Filipetti had worked with Sony Music on multi-channel SACD projects more than a decade earlier and knew the DSW team well; their experience had overlapped on projects with artists such as Simon, Desmond Child, and Courtney Love.

And he was nearby: always an advantage with a tight schedule. One of the first record producers to commit to digital techniques, Filipetti had set up a professional studio in his home in West Nyack, New York, just north of the city. They ended up recording about one-third of the tracks for 4TROOPS' CD there and the rest at various studios in Manhattan. "When you work this way, all the mixing is done later in the computer," he says. "I can get all the sound data on a hard drive, do the mixes at home, and send it back, or sometimes send material over the internet."

Filipetti was instantly engaged by the group members as people but also by the professional challenge. "There are two really exciting things you get to do in your career," he believes. "One is to work with someone you've always admired, a musical hero, and to enter into a relationship with him or her—like James Taylor or Carly Simon. But it's equally exciting to work with an artist no one knows. Two months earlier, this group didn't exist, but I could tell they had something special. There was the opportunity to help mold their sound, that chance to be part of something that breaks out of nowhere."

Above: 4TROOPS confer with record producer Frank Filipetti at Downtown Recording Studios in Manhattan. Overleaf: Behind the scenes during the "Four Freedom" music video shoot at Downtown Recording Studios.

A producer's job is much like a film director's, says Filipetti: choosing the studio locations, hiring the production staff and musicians, putting together concepts for sound and musical direction, laying out a recording plan, overseeing and/or creating arrangements, and in most cases choosing repertoire. "In this case, most of the songs were already picked by the time I got involved at the end of 2009, but we had discussions around the last four," he says.

Even before the recording sessions, which were spread over February and March, there was lots of ground to cover. While the 4TROOPS were home on holiday breaks, Fili-

petti, Hurtado, and Sony Music's David Lai looked over and tinkered with some of the early arrangements the group had been using. MIDI and MP3 files of songs being considered flew back and forth in cyberspace. Filipetti assembled his team, starting with star arranger Rob Mounsey, who quickly became involved in the process, building instrumental support around the vocal lines.

"The process was mostly driven by the time it took to get arrangements done," notes Lai. Songs were recorded as arrangements were readied, sometimes one at a time. In between, Lai rehearsed the group so they would be prepared by the time they went into the studio. "Because I was conducting *Phantom*, we sometimes rehearsed in the Majestic Theatre on 45th Street (where the show played)—there's a big lower lobby space we could use during the day, and it was free!"

Simultaneously, of course, Lai was prepping 4TROOPS for their big live concert on the *Intrepid*. Lai engaged Tony Award-nominated choreographer Christopher Gattelli—the two had worked together on the Tony Award-winning *South Pacific* production at Lincoln Center—to create and teach staging and choreography for the *Intrepid* concert. "The work Chris did was brilliant. He had to come up with something that was exciting and added a dynamic element to the performance, yet was simple enough to learn quickly and not distract from the message of the music. And I knew the group would respond immediately to his energy."

"We were playing catch-up every minute," recalls Winston Simone. "They were learning as they were recording, and then it would be, 'Oh my God, they have to sing the national anthem next week!'"

Both in rehearsing and recording the group, the main challenge was blend. "Here

114

were four people with incredible solo voices," says Filipetti. "Each had a lot of range, the ability to emote, the ability to create a recording. What they needed to work on was singing as a unit. I related it to what they had to do in the military in basic training."

This didn't mean a uniform, drill-team approach to singing. Indeed, Lai and Filipetti coached the 4TROOPS on how to inhabit and "own" a song, including work on diction, projecting, and focus of expression. "These aren't just pop songs, they carry stories and messages, and getting the words across is essential for their emotional impact," says Lai. "You're trying to inspire, motivate and help people, convey the central idea of hope. The song's intent is driven partly by the melodic line but just as much by the words." Lai sometimes had them just speak the lyrics at first to absorb their meaning, "and then we'd talk about how to personalize the song for them."

Sooner than anyone thought possible, the group met with Filipetti in the studio for the first time. "Normally you have lots of preproduction time to work on songs with a band—at least a month or two. You go into a studio and record a little, try different things, play around. Plus, the band members usually have performed together a lot and probably recorded before." None of that applied. "They were so nervous," Filipetti recalls.

"They said, 'We've never done this before—what if we don't live up to what's expected?'" Trying to lighten things up, he replied, "Funny you should say that . . . I get really nervous when someone shoots off a gun at me!" He reassured them, "If we make a mistake in the studio, nobody dies. You guys have the talent to pull this off; you're going to do this."

Recording fifteen cuts in less than two months was still a tall order. Not only did the 4TROOPS have to learn the songs, in some cases they had to unlearn versions they already knew. "My idea was, if it's a cover, I wanted a new perspective on it," says Filipetti. "I didn't want it to sound like the Sarah [McLachlan] or the Luther [Vandross] or the Lonestar version." The singers had to learn challenging lead vocal lines in some cases, and in others, complicated harmonies created for them. "Rob and I did vocal arrangements for thirteen of the fifteen, starting from scratch, writing out all the parts," says Filipetti. "But we couldn't add the instrumental parts until we heard how the arrangements worked in their vocal ranges. So we used mostly computer arrangements at the beginning." Once he heard what the group did at this stage, he could adjust keys, tempo, and vocal assignments as needed. "And sometimes even though we came in with arrangements I could alter things on the fly, in the studio."

Filipetti chose the first song to record, "I'm Already There," because it relies on individual vocal lines for a much of its length before the harmonies come in. "It was a good song to get the 4TROOPS used to the process." Part of that first day was also devoted to teaching the singers how to lay down harmony parts. "I put them in front of four different microphones, and started them getting used to hearing themselves through headphones—that's a whole other science. Your voice is right in your ear; you're hearing things you've never heard before, and it's hard to hear the pitch or know whether you're over-emoting." It was a hard day, but successful, he says.

On day two, Filipetti played back the first track for them. "And I think they suddenly realized, maybe this will work. Later that day we did a few takes of 'Broken Road,' and they literally nailed it. That gave them more confidence, and from there on everything went about as well as it could have."

As the sessions moved on, Filipetti continued the singers' vocal education, from a recording perspective. "There was so much they had to learn and that I had to learn about them. Recognizing the rhythmic directions each person tends to take, so that when they're following a lead, they know where to go. Really listening all

> I told them, if we make a mistake in the studio, nobody dies. You're going to do this.
>
> —Frank Filipetti, Producer

around instead of just concentrating on your own vocal. Being able to emotional-ize as a group: create the same vibe in a certain part of a song. Thinking about the dynamic arc of a song: where the musical climaxes and the emotional climaxes fall." At the same time they were learning to be recording artists, they also had to become

> ## They suddenly realized, maybe this will work.
>
> —FRANK FILIPETTI, PRODUCER

stage performers. "Like actors who have to adjust from being subtle on a movie screen to more obvious in a big theater space, they needed to know when to reach a little harder with something onstage versus holding back on a recording.

"Suddenly they're not just playing a guitar with friends but singing in front of thou-sands at Yankee Stadium, or in a room full of critical people with headphones on," Fili-petti adds. "But they were so eager to learn that within a few short intense weeks they had moved leaps and bounds. Within six weeks of joining together as a group, they were onstage playing all fifteen songs in concert, and in the middle of recording them. Learn-ing movements, timing, lyrics, all in such a compressed time frame."

On a typical day of recording, 4TROOPS would spend half the day recording a lead vocal, sometimes trading off. "We'd get that all the way done, then do the background harmonies," says Filipetti. Which at first could be a little rocky. Filipetti had the option of having them sing parts individually and then combine them in the mix, sing all the harmony lines together, or record two plus two, and he used each option for different songs. "As they got more used to blending with headphones on, they could sing together more often." He also arranged for each singer to have his/her own headphone box with a unique mix in their ear, so each could hear what worked best for them. "They became studio pros so much quicker than I or they or Sony Music would ever have expected."

To say that the results thrilled the whole team is the simple truth. Alex Miller of Sony MASTERWORKS believes that "the way the songs hang together in sequencing is a credit to Frank's genius in arranging and skill in working with the group's vocal gifts." All the cuts are individually strong as well as building an emotional journey overall—but the team members do single out cuts that evoke special associations.

For Victor Hurtado, it's "Courtesy of the Red, White, and Blue." David Simoné felt that the album needed that song's energy and fire, but Hurtado and the 4TROOPS were uncomfortable with some of Toby Keith's more in-your-face lyrics—the song, after all, was his emotional response to 9/11. Simoné suggested that Hurtado write alternate lyrics for Keith's approval, and though he thought it was a long shot, Hurtado tried it. He sent

the new lyrics off at Christmastime, and in February heard from DSW that Keith had given them his blessing. "I thought that was an incredible gesture and showed how true his support is for our military," Hurtado says, "especially given how personal the song was for him."

For Winston Simone, "Bless the Broken Road" was a perfect song for the group, with its country roots and message of a survivor's gratitude. Songwriter Marcus Hummon had heard many versions of his song—on a Nitty Gritty Dirt Band album and a hit version in 2004 by Rascal Flatts—but he was excited to learn that it would be recorded by four combat veterans, with Frank Filipetti at the controls. "I could hear the excitement in David and Winston's voices when they talked to me about the group," he says. "They sent me a rough mix, which was lovely. David's lead singing at times reminds me of Gary Levox of Rascal Flatts, but then shifts into a more bluesy place." Hummon hosted 4TROOPS when they came to Nashville. "They came to my house the evening before. Ron sat right down at the piano and started playing 'Broken Road' in his churchy mode. They all started out very quiet and respectful, and I was trying to draw them out. Finally I brought out some wine, and it turned into a long evening of singing Beatles songs and everything else."

Two songs stand out for Filipetti. About "Dance with My Father," he says, "Here's a classic that had been performed by one of the world's great singers. Luther's version is so locked in your mind that it's intimidating even to another great singer. I gave Ron a little direction about where to lighten up or get more emotional—especially trying to get him to find the joy in it—but from the first time he started singing, I said, 'This is Ron's version.' He really comes through on this song, a guy who for twenty years was carrying a rifle in the Army. Right up there with Luther."

> They became studio pros so much quicker than I or they or Sony would ever have expected.
>
> —FRANK FILIPETTI, PRODUCER

Above: *4TROOPS with songwriter Marcus Hummon at Hummon's home in Nashville.*

"I Dream of Galveston"

Midway through the 4TROOPS CD, a gentle guitar intro takes us into one of the great country-pop songs ever written: Jimmy Webb's "Galveston." It's Daniel Jens' big moment on the album, and he makes the most of it with a vocal performance full of raw longing, backed up with haunting minor-key harmonies by the other group members.

Named by CMT as one of the Top Ten country music songs of all time, "Galveston" was a major hit single for Glen Campbell in 1969. Because it appeared just as the Vietnam War was peaking, the song became irrevocably associated with that conflict—and many people read antiwar sentiments into it. In fact, the basis for the its storyline was Webb imagining a young U.S. soldier in the Spanish-American War of 1898 thinking of his hometown. Most who love the song today feel that the timeless lyric could apply to a soldier of any era, from the Civil War to Iraq, where Jens served.

"When that song came up as a candidate," says Alex Miller, "I remembered listening to it on AM radio. Of all the Vietnam-era songs, it was to me the perfect embodiment of a soldier's longing and desire for home, his attachment to a place almost like a lover."

Music director David Lai thinks this was an especially important song for the featured vocalist to inhabit and own. "Knowing Dan's history of going to war, and what was important to him—his wife and child—he had to hold that in mind while he was singing. It's not just about someplace called Galveston; you're singing about your own home and loved ones."

Not long after the CD appeared, Jimmy Webb himself gave Jens' performance the ultimate shout-out. In an online interview promoting his new album "Just Across the River" (Webb performing his hits with stellar guest artists), he declares, "my guy [in the song] was just an ordinary guy from Galveston who misses home." Going on, he says, "The song was just recorded by this group called 4TROOPS, and the guy who sings it says [quoting Jens from the *Intrepid* concert], 'Everything you described in that song, I went through in Iraq: I watch the cannon flashing, and I clean my gun . . .'

Webb pauses briefly in the interview, visibly choking up. "And man, when he said that, it got a hold of me," he finally continues. "You know, sometimes when you're writing things ... it's not all in your control. There are times when there are other things at work."

For his part, Jens says simply, "I'm so grateful to have had my chance with this incredible song. It's been a way to kind of connect with an earlier generation of soldiers that were listening to it when it first came out. To think about a soldier in Vietnam, maybe with a guitar, singing 'Galveston' for his buddies—that's an amazing feeling." ★

The other was Meredith doing "Angel." It was her big moment, "a perfect, iconic song, and I've never seen anyone more nervous," Filipetti remembers. She said, 'I just don't think I can do this,' and the first time through I could hear a little strain in her voice, just not totally comfortable." But by the second or third time through, her performance moved him to tears. "I put a nice mix on it and played it for her the next day. She listened, petrified, and them came and hugged me and my assistant Derek. But I said, 'That was all you.'"

David Lai is partial to the patriotic medley of "Grand Old Flag," "America the Beautiful," and "God Bless America." "I thought those arrangements were very well done, very clever," he says. "My first reaction was that those kinds of songs might make the album feel dowdy, but the arrangements are very contemporary." The group members themselves aren't picking favorites, aside from their big solo numbers.

The self-titled debut CD was released on May 11, 2010—two weeks ahead of the original projected date. Sony Music chose to release the album during Armed Forces Week (May 8 to May 15), which honors Americans serving in all five services: Army, Navy, Marines, Air Force, and Coast Guard. 4TROOPS made another whirlwind round of the talk shows that week though Memorial Day, with appearances on *Huckabee*, *Good Morning America*, *Larry King Live*, *Fox & Friends*, *CBS Saturday Early Show*, the *Laura Ingraham Show*, and ABC's *The View* and *Nightline*. The CD briefly shot up to #2 on Amazon, then settled into strong sales more in line with a debut album. "The album debuted very

Above: *4TROOPS with producer Frank Filipetti at Downtown Recording Studios in Manhattan.*

high for an unknown group," says Alex Miller. "Internet sales were astounding—it was the #8 internet album on debut week, which is a great indicator of performance especially in rural America. People have been motivated to get their hands on it, so it's clearly striking a chord with listeners."

As gratifying as the results were, it's the road to the record that the principals remember best, and the relationships forged along the way. Chalk that up to the spirit and grit and talent of the group. As the consummate professional David Lai notes, "Working in the music industry for so long, you can forget that it's really a pretty thrilling business. Every step was special because everything was new to them: the first time meeting the arranger, the first time going into the studio. It was fun to be on that journey with them."

Producer Frank Filipetti by now regards 4TROOPS as family. "When I first met them, I realized that, apart from being enamored of people who risk their lives to defend us, they happened to be terrific people as well." His wife, Ellie Filipetti, adopted them as well, baking for them during recording sessions and posting kudos on the 4TROOPS Facebook page with each new milestone the group hit.

Filipetti sees the album as "a tribute not only to what these kids can do—I still think of them as kids—but to what they learned in their military service. They are amazing in their dedication, their ability to connect with people, to be the best they can be. Whether you're for or against any particular war, these are people who did something few of us are willing to do." He believes that their dedication and ambition, aided by the "incredible support" of DSW and Sony Music, give them a chance to make a real mark. "And if this doesn't become a monster success, it's still one of my favorite things I've ever done.

"When David and Winston first said they were looking for an 'inspirational album,' I had to think about that," he says. "Those can so often be overdone or sappy. We tried to capture the simplicity of a great song with some tasty sweetening—to make an honest, upfront signature of these people, so that the emotion of the singer and what they're saying comes through. And these kids did it." ★

They are amazing in their dedication, their ability to connect with people, to be the best they can be.

—FRANK FILIPETTI, PRODUCER

The way we're being treated now is because of what the guys in Vietnam went through, what the guys who were in Korea went through, what the guys who were in World War II went through . . . So to be able to give back to those who laid the groundwork for us—to them and to others who are going to get out later with injuries or other issues—I couldn't ask for more or be more proud.
—DAVID CLEMO

Part 3

FORWARD DEPLOYMENT

Taking It on the Road

"So when do we start booking this?!" Back in December 2009, as 4TROOPS finished the last song in their crucial showcase audition for Sony MASTER-WORKS label, the first reaction from the crowded room was that question by Andrea Johnson. An agent in the New York office of The Agency Group, an international firm that does tour bookings for leading musical artists in many genres, she was on hand because Sony Music wanted their early impression of 4TROOPS' potential—not just on record but in person.

Johnson's "let's get started" reflex was the answer. "Conceptually there was no way this wasn't going to work," Johnson declares. "The climate in America was right, people are hungry for something this authentic. And we've got four extraordinary human beings who also happen to sing like angels. How fortuitous was that combination?"

Taking the music on road is a rite of passage (not to mention a commercial necessity) for any new group. There's no substitute for the passions and the bond created between performers and a living, breathing audience. And these days the public's focus is pulled in every direction. "Because our attention is so fragmented, you have to get your message out over and over," says Sony MASTERWORKS' Alex Miller. "What we've found with 4TROOPS is an incredible immediacy of response to them, from different demographic groups all over the country."

> There's been a lot of talk about honoring veterans . . . but now we're assigning faces to the concept, and their stories are real.
>
> —ANDREA JOHNSON, BOOKING AGENT

That augured well for a tour, and planning began for one as soon as the group was signed. But how do you book concerts for a group no one has heard yet? A conventional model, harking back to the days when a large proportion of records were sold at con-

certs, is to have a group's tour coincide with the release of a new album. Since 4TROOPS' debut CD wasn't released until May 2010, they wouldn't have had enough exposure yet to support a tour, so a different strategy was called for. "When we learned that PBS was part of the equation, the direction became clear," says Johnson.

"It's an approach that builds around a live performance airing on many public television stations, and the artist's appearances on TV and in other media," she explains. "There's kind of a formula to the timing: you need to wait a certain amount of time for viewers to see and respond to the artist, and for other stations to react to how things go. Once you've gained some traction, it can snowball." The PBS special *4TROOPS: Live from the Intrepid* aired throughout June, "traditionally the slowest of the three annual pledge drives," Johnson notes. "But we've heard from many stations that the response to 4TROOPS has been strong and very positive."

4TROOPS did their part to make sure of that. In early June the group members hit the road to help promote the special at stations around the country. They split up, Daniel Jens and Ron Henry visiting San Diego, San Antonio, Tampa, Atlanta (where Henry got to greet his mom on the air), Raleigh-Durham, Pittsburgh, Milwaukee, Hartford, and Nashville. David Clemo and Meredith Melcher were dispatched to Albuquerque, Lincoln (Nebraska), Sacramento, Fresno, Kansas City, Columbus (Ohio), and Roanoke, Virginia. They performed cuts from the CD, told their stories live on air during pledge breaks, and even answered phones, spreading the word to PBS supporters. "I spoke with someone who remembered me from *America's Got Talent*," says Jens, "so that was a thrill."

Even before this, the group had gotten their performing feet wet with a mini-tour in May of U.S. Army installations, where they could try out their chops in front of audiences predisposed to respond warmly. They appeared at Andrews Air Force Base in Camp Spring, Maryland; Fort Sam Houston in San Antonio and Fort Hood, in Texas; and at Fort Eustis and Harbourfest in the

Above, left: Jens and Henry joke around with Sesame Street's Cookie Monster at PBS station UNC-TV in North Carolina. Above, right: Melcher and Clemo work the phones at WNPT-TV in Nashville. Opposite: 4TROOPS perform at Fort Sam Houston, Texas.

Norfolk, Virginia. These shows gave them a preview of the emotional bonds they hope to forge with fans in every live setting. David Clemo especially remembers a moment during their concert at Andrews. "We were singing, 'I'm Already There,' and Daniel and I both noticed a mother and daughter singing along and hugging each other, and the little girl was crying." It was easy for them to imagine the family's situation, "but we weren't ready for that reaction," says Clemo.

The group continued to play a few more gigs through summer 2010, with stops in Springfield, Ohio; Long Island; Florida; Reno, Nevada; and West Allis, Wisconsin. In September the pace picked up dramatically, with concerts in fifty-plus locations scheduled to the end of the year. Venues ran the gamut from midsize auditoriums to state fairs to Indian gaming resorts, plus a few fundraisers for veterans' causes. Putting the tour together posed the usual logistical challenges, says Andrea Johnson—for instance, trying to cluster events in a region rather than making the group yo-yo back and forth across the country. In general she targeted major markets and places where the group had made station visits first, filling in the spaces between.

"But one of the most exciting things about 4TROOPS," says Johnson, "is that the middle-size and smaller markets are just as important as New York City, if not more so. That's where you're reaching Americans of all kinds." And unlike with other emerging artists, who may not play well in heartland areas, "exactly the opposite is true here. There just aren't any places we have to avoid, and their appeal has been just as strong in so-called 'blue' parts of the country." While some acts she has worked with are totally dependent on the PBS connection, that's not true of 4TROOPS. "There's lots of love for them in general, because of their compelling stories."

Beyond building a schedule, planning for the tour extended into all corners of 4TROOPS' world. Music director David Lai worked on their stage presentation and vocal projection, quite a different set of skills than they needed for recording. Their stage wardrobe had to be planned and assembled: "It was important that they look like soldiers in every detail," says DSW's Winston Simone, but it was also important that, as veterans, they did not wear current active-duty uniforms—especially when visiting military installations.

> So many of our fans are veterans or their families. It means so much to be singing for them.
>
> —DANIEL JENS

A key decision early on was that they would not tour with a band. "Once you put a band on the road it requires another whole substructure of management," says producer Frank Filipetti. "But mainly we wanted to keep it simple for the group their first time out. So they don't have to worry about whether the drums are too loud one night, or the guitars are out of tune, or whatever. Just let them get their live playing chops together without those distractions."

This meant that every arrangement created for 4TROOPS had to be reproducible with live voices. They do all their own singing, but with a track instead of a live band behind them. "And the track has to sound great in performance, not just on record," Filipetti notes. For media appearances and smaller stages, he provided the basic recording tracks as a stereo mix without vocals. For the main tour, however, he created "stems"—that is, a stereo mix of each element: drums, bass, guitars, keyboards. "Then the live mixer for the show can adjust those levels separately, depending on the sound in each venue."

One innovation 4TROOPS introduced for the fall tour was a short acoustic set that featured some new songs and showed off their instrumental prowess: Jens and Clemo played guitar and Henry and Melcher took turns at the piano. They also performed the bonus track "Amazing Grace."

Preparing for a major tour was one more big step the 4TROOPS have taken in stride. "It boggles the mind how easily they've taken to it all," says Johnson. When she first described her role to them, and what it would mean to be on the road for months, "they

were so excited and happy," she recalls. She warned them, however, that their enthusiasm might fray around the edges after weeks of touring. "I said, somewhere around Tulsa six weeks into this thing, you're going to be using my face as a dartboard!"

For now, the 4TROOPS remain upbeat about going on the road, even the mundane aspects. They travel in a spiffy luxury tour bus, "like a motel on wheels," Jens reports. All of them look forward to stops in places where they have lived, so that family and friends can attend concerts and catch up with them. They also recognize that some personal hardships lie ahead. David Clemo, in particular, winces at the thought of being apart from his new baby daughter and her mother.

But they all recognize how important these concerts around America have been in promoting their goals. "I want as many people as possible to hear us because I want them to feel the love and the camaraderie throughout this whole project," says Ron Henry. Jens says, "What I'm most looking forward to is singing in front of our fans in packed theaters. So many of our fans are veterans, family of veterans or active duty. It means so much to be singing for them." Meredith Melcher looks forward "to meeting those people who have supported us throughout this entire project. They are the reason we are successful enough to even have a tour, so my priority is doing my absolute best to make it a show that is worth their time and money. " For Clemo, "This has a purpose and that is what makes it great. Joann [his fiancée] and I are willing to deal with the separation because of the message and vibe of the whole project."

Judging from the excited postings on the group's website and Facebook page, Americans are waiting eagerly to experience 4TROOPS in person. "Talk about one of the largest groups of disenfranchised people!" Andrea Johnson exclaims. "There's been a lot of talk about honoring veterans, and talk is cheap. But now," she says, "we're assigning faces to the concept of helping veterans, and most important, their stories are real. Americans are sick of fakery, and they recognize the 4TROOPS as authentic, something that can really touch their lives. And what better way to do it than through song?" ★

Above left: *Jens and Henry with early copies of the* Live from the Intrepid *concert DVD.*
Above right: *4TROOPS with General David H. Petraeus on the* Intrepid.

Angel Voices

"It's great to hear artists who have actually lived through family separation and all the other aspects of war sing about it. I was getting tired of hearing superstars singing about something that they really don't have any idea about. Thank you, 4TROOPS!" said one Facebook fan.

The love affair that has bloomed between 4TROOPS and their fans, like the writer above, is unique in today's popular music scene. Like other groups, 4TROOPS uses 21st-century social networking tools to spread the word about what they're doing, make personal contact, and invite feedback—but the people they reach out to (and vice versa) are a different breed from the typical starstruck pop acolyte. They are young, old, and everything in between; male and female, sons, daughters, parents, grandparents. And many of them have come to see the group as family.

That "family" is the far-flung yet tightly knit community of Americans who have a connection with the armed services. They are active-duty soldiers, some of whom even served with members of 4TROOPS and write to cheer them on. They are veterans, many from the Iraq and Afghanistan conflicts, but going back as far as World War II. They are the spouses of soldiers and veterans from every branch of the service, or their mothers, fathers, sisters, brothers, and every other relation you can think of. They are young people about to enlist or get their commissions. Some are just Americans who haven't forgotten our history of human sacrifice in the cause of this country's highest and best values.

And they recognize the real deal when they see and hear it. Military service, especially combat duty, is a badge of honor not to be worn without cause, as some public figures have learned. Their fans know that the members of 4TROOPS are all combat veterans of Iraq and Afghanistan (whether or not they came under fire); that they all served honorably; and that even before the group existed, each used his or her musical talents in the service of other soldiers. As they have discovered 4TROOPS' music and learned about its mission—whether on a talk show, by catching the PBS special, attending a live show, or hearing a friend rave about them—they've responded by downloading or buying the physical CD (often in multiples as gifts), ordering concert tickets, spreading the word among their families and friends, and expressing their gratitude for what 4TROOPS is doing in hundreds of posts to the group's website and Facebook fan page. At this writing the Facebook fan total stands at more than 10,000, an extraordinary figure for a new group.

The keynote struck in all these messages, in myriad ways, is "Thank you!" The fans love 4TROOPS' music, admire their great voices and sweet harmonies, and talk about how the songs affect them: evoking joy, pride, and often tears. They appreciate the group's up-front profession of patriotism and faith, hail their service, and applaud the way they are bringing veterans' issues to public attention.

And they take the opportunity to tell stories of their own. Many are military mothers who proudly name their loved ones who served or are serving. Kathy posted on the 4TROOPS website: "I heard 4TROOPS sing for the first time this morning. I was so moved by their voices and the words of their song. I am a Marine mom, missing my 21 year old daughter very much this Memorial Day weekend. My little girl is a veteran of Iraq, currently deployed to Afghanistan. As I listened intently, I felt my sadness lifting." Says ArmyBandMom, "My husband served in Korea and our son now serves in the Army the past ten years. He is a sixth-generation military and our only child. When he left for Iraq it took all we had to get through it.... So tonight when we watched 4TROOPS on PBS it brought such joy, and tears fell as you sang each song. You were so right when you spoke about separation. Seeing your faith, hearing your beautiful voices touched our hearts."

4TROOPS keep in touch with their fans as much as their busy schedule allows. They take turns posting general greetings on Facebook as well as replying to some individual messages. Says Meredith Melcher: "The audience response has been so overwhelmingly positive that I truly feel humbled. We get so many emails and Facebook messages from people who have listened to our music and feel uplifted or inspired. And it's not just the military community who supports us; a lot of civilians have taken an interest in our mission."

Ron Henry posted in early June: "From the bottom of our hearts, we send out our continual thanks for all your support. We would not be here without you. Peace & Love." From Daniel Jens around the same time: "Thank you to all who joined after watching *Nightline* and *The View*! We appreciate all our fans so much." And David Clemo writes, "I want to thank all of you that have served. Anyone that is a family member of someone who has served . . . thanks for your service too. You make it possible for the people in our armed forces to stay focused and get home safe. That is the toughest job in the military!"

Another way that 4TROOPS gives back to veterans and their families is in the tangible form of financial donations: $.50 from the sale of each CD by Sony Music in the United States is being donated to groups that support veterans and their families.

The donations will be divided equally among The American Legion, Iraq and Afghanistan Veterans of America (IAVA), Intrepid Fallen Heroes Fund, and the USO. Both fans and the groups they support express gratitude for this gesture. The four organizations work through military and home communities on a wide range of programs, and each takes a different approach. (See page 143 for more information about each.)

The groups involved in this program appreciate 4TROOPS' help in bringing their issues before the public. Says IAVA Executive Director Paul Rieckhoff, "4TROOPS is an inspiring band composed of new veterans and leaders of this generation. They are using music to draw on their wartime experience, boost troop morale, and rally Americans in support of service members."

Just as it is to their fan base, 4TROOPS' authenticity was important to these groups and their large constituencies. "It was always key to our plans to build these connections," says Sony MASTERWORKS' Alex Miller, "and the groups involved had to know and believe that 4TROOPS were for real." Everyone on the 4TROOPS team who has worked on these partnerships has been struck by the groups' devotion to their cause. Winston Simone of DSW Entertainment says, "You wish that every society was as dedicated to helping each other as these people are."

Beyond these partner organizations, 4TROOPS has also supported veterans-related projects with benefit appearances. One of these is the Jericho Project, a New York-based group that is currently developing two new supportive housing residences for homeless and low-income veterans in the Bronx—the first new housing programs for veterans in New York City in fifteen years. In April, 4TROOPS played at a Jericho fundraiser at the Chelsea Piers. "We played our Patriotic Medley," recalled David Clemo, "and I got to talk to some vets at that event, people who had become quite successful and were involved with this amazing effort. I think they raised something like $600,000 that night."

To those who have come to know 4TROOPS—in person, on record, through their warm presence onstage and online, or through their generous support of veterans' causes—they are angels. And to the group, these members of their extended family, military and civilian alike, are equally a blessing. The unique bonds they have forged with their fans are summed up by Tracy Nolan. She writes, "All I can say is . . . thank you!! I saw your special on PBS, and cried and laughed and finally believed that there is life after war. Your stories and angelic voices are a true inspiration to all of us." ★

> It's not just the military community who supports us; a lot of civilians have taken an interest in our mission.
> —MEREDITH MELCHER

Drive On!

"**We always say that our mission is to honor** and raise awareness for those that have served and are currently serving, as well as their family members. But sometimes putting a face to a situation can make all the difference between words and actions, and that day I believe it truly did."

One Sunday in June, Former Cpt. Meredith Melcher lost it. "It was our second day of shows at Harbourfest in Norfolk [VA], and we were about to take the stage," she relates. "We noticed a man and a woman talking to someone on the event staff over by the sidelines, and it looked like they were asking about meeting us. Since we had a few minutes before we had to go on, we went over and said hello." The couple said they were fans, then told the 4TROOPS that their son, Marine Sgt. Jayton Patterson, had been killed while serving in Afghanistan. "They were wearing shirts with his name printed on the back.

"We decided we would dedicate the show to him, announcing it right after we sang 'You Raise Me Up.'" As they went onstage, Melcher noticed the Pattersons sitting in lawn chairs near the front. Their second song was Meredith's solo number "Angel." "Right after I finished the first verse and chorus, I looked down at Jayton's mom. I just wanted to briefly acknowledge her in a friendly way, but that simple act of looking at her made me break down in tears. In a split second, emotion came rushing into me so fast that it took me by complete surprise. I was literally wracked with sobs. It wasn't as if I started to well up and begin crying; this was instantaneous grief."

Unable to sing, Melcher looked desperately toward the other group members to take over, but they were occupied with their own vocals. Turning away from the audience, she continued to loudly sob, unable to pull it together. "I remember being shocked at myself, because I am typically very calm and unshakable, especially on stage, but now I couldn't control my emotions. When I looked at Jayton's mom, I wasn't even consciously associating her son's death with the song lyrics, but in the moment the emotion hit me, all I could think about was the lines I had just sung: 'You're in the arms of the angel, may you find some comfort here.'

"When I realized I wouldn't be able to go on singing any time soon, I figured I might as well try to explain my emotion." She spoke to the audience, telling them what she knew about Jayton's sacrifice and asking that the audience recognize his parents. "Jayton's mom and dad stood up and waved. Everyone was clapping and showing their support." After that, she managed to take a few breaths and resume singing. "There were maybe forty-five seconds left in the song, and though I sounded like a complete wreck, I managed to shakily squeak it out." Melcher remained on the emotional edge for the rest of the day, even asking if she could skip "Angel" during the second show because she was afraid tears would overtake her again.

"Now that I've had time to reflect on it," she says, "I think I reacted that way because I realized that Jayton and his parents are the purest examples of why 4TROOPS is doing what we are doing. We always tell people that our mission is to essentially honor and raise awareness for those that have served and are currently serving our country, as well as their family members. So hearing Jayton's parents tell their story right before we went onstage struck a really deep chord."

Most vocalists are familiar with the balancing act required to let emotions enrich their performance without allowing themselves to be vocally undone by them. More than most, the members of 4TROOPS have to walk this line on a regular basis—and this time, after stress-filled months of learning, rehearsing, recording, talking to the media, and performing around the country, Meredith fell off. But she'll learn from the experience and forge on, as will all of the group members: far from their homes and families over the coming months of touring, relying on each other for support and continuing to connect personally with their growing legion of fans.

"We sing together like we're family. We act like we're family. It's in line with the Army motto: We take care of our own," as Ron explains it. "That's what we've been doing since we came together. We take care of one another. We encourage one another. We give constructive criticism to one another—all to help bring out our best."

To those close to the group it's clear that their past service does inform their present mission in a big way. "It's those memories and personal relationships with servicemen and women and families that get them up every day," believes Alex Miller. "They won't ever forget the experience of serving, and of course each still has friends and colleagues who are on active duty. It just makes them great models for teamwork.

"The other beautiful thing to see has been the camaraderie among them," Miller adds. "They really see themselves as a group, are democratic in their decision-making and unified in their approach. Of course there are emphatic discussions

> We sing together like we're family. We act like we're family. It's in line with the Army motto: We take care of our own.
>
> —Ron Henry

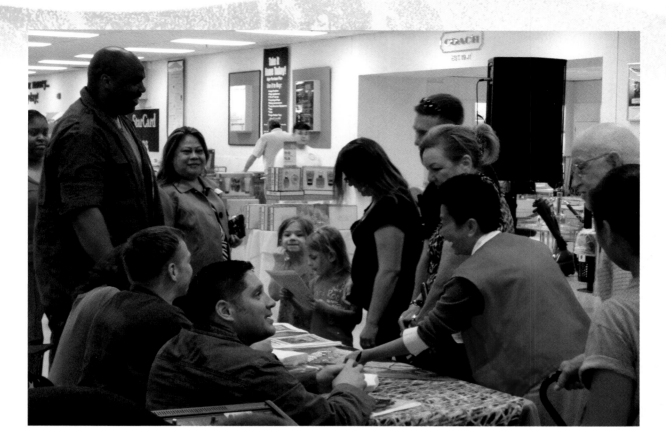

about how to get the message across, but they always get to unity. They know from experience that the group is stronger than any individual."

For these reasons and more, there's a strong sense that 4TROOPS will endure and flourish. No one is trying to peer too far into the future, but the performers and their team look forward to introducing subtle changes in their repertoire and presentation over time: certainly new songs, perhaps original material, maybe touring with a band the next time out. Topping the list of goals for the 4TROOPS themselves is touring to the war zones in Iraq and Afghanistan. "We've talked about that a lot among ourselves," says Meredith Melcher, "and mentioned to management that it's a primary goal of ours, because those are the people who need it the most."

On behalf of the group, Melcher reminds us that it's all been about giving thanks and giving back. "I would have done myself an injustice—and my country and the people I served with an injustice—not to use what was given me to be a part of the solution, to help soldiers get through that next week or next month, and then bring it back home.

"If you give of yourself, eventually it will come back to you. I feel like our opportunity to become 4TROOPS has come back to us in that way. It's a dream being fulfilled, and abundantly more." ★

Above: 4TROOPS sign posters for Army family members at Fort Sam Houston, Texas.

We are 4TROOPS

The mighty mighty 4TROOPS!

Partners for the Troops

Sony Music will donate 50 cents from each sale of the 4TROOPS album in the United States to organizations that support veterans and their families. That donation will be split equally among the following organizations:

The American Legion, the nation's largest military veterans organization, was founded in 1919 on the four pillars of a strong national security, veterans affairs, Americanism, and youth programs. Legionnaires work to better their communities through more than 14,000 posts across the nation. **www.legion.org**

IAVA is the nation's first and largest nonprofit nonpartisan group dedicated to bettering the lives of Iraq and Afghanistan veterans and their families. **www.iava.org**

Intrepid Fallen Heroes Fund (IFHF) has raised over $120 million in support for the families of military personnel lost in service to our nation, and for severely wounded military personnel and veterans. The Fund most recently opened the National Intrepid Center of Excellence to support the research, diagnosis, and treatment of traumatic brain injury. **www.fallenheroesfund.org**

The **USO** delivers programs and services to millions of active-duty troops, National Guard, and Reserves, as well as their families, at more than 150 centers worldwide. Services include free Internet and e-mail access, libraries and reading rooms, housing assistance, family crisis counseling, support groups, game rooms, and nursery facilities. The USO also produces hundreds of entertainment shows around the world each year. **www.uso.org**

Acknowledgments & Credits

Newmarket Press extends deepest thanks to all who generously contributed information, interviews, photographs, and other assistance that made this book possible, especially:

At DSW Entertainment: David Simoné, Winston Simone, Dexter Scott Robison, and Kirsten Schubert

At Sony MASTERWORKS: Alex Miller, Laura Kszan, David Lai, Angela Barkan, Larissa Slezak, Tara Bruh, Jennifer Liebeskind, Roxanne Slimak, and Karen Cunningham

Victor M. Hurtado (C*A*M*M*O Center for American Military Music Opportunities), Tim Hipps (Senior Information Specialist with the U.S. Army Family and Morale, Welfare and Recreation Command Public Affairs Office), Andrea Johnson of The Agency Group, Paul Rieckhoff of IAVA, Frank Filipetti, Shelley Ross, Lt. Gen. (Ret.) David Melcher, Noel Campbell, and Ryan Barkan

And most especially our favorite troops: Former Cpt. Meredith Melcher, Former Sgt. Daniel Jens, Staff Sgt. (Ret.) Ron D. Henry, and Former Sgt. David Clemo

Photography: Jimmy Asnes/Sony Music Entertainment, pages 2–3, 6, 14–15, 16, 19, 20–21, 22, 32, 42, 52, 63-64, 75, 86–87, 90–91, 95, 97, 98–99, 108, 111, 112–113, 114, 115, 116–117, 121, 123, 126, 132, 136, 140–141; Ryan Barkan, pages 104–105, 106, 107; Richard Corman/Sony Music Entertainment, pages 10, 29, 39, 49, 57, 84, 85, 109; Tim Hipps/U.S. Army FMWRC Public Affairs, pages 51, 66, 68, 74, 76, 78, 92, 93; Bob Hoch/Sony Music Entertainment, pages 102, 103; Alex Miller/Sony Music Entertainment, page 65; Dexter Scott Robison, pages 80–83, 101, 120, 128, 129, 131, 139; "Sesame Workshop"®, "Sesame Street"®, and associated characters, trademarks, and design elements are owned and licensed by Sesame Workshop. © 2010 Sesame Workshop. All Rights Reserved, page 128; Tom Whitmore/ Getty Images for NASCAR, page 100; U.S. Army FMWRC Entertainment Division, pages 67, 69; U.S. Government Press, pages 70, 73; Courtesy of Meredith Melcher, pages 12, 24–28, 94 ; Courtesy of Daniel Jens, pages 12, 34–36, 38, 41; Courtesy of Ron D. Henry, pages 13, 44–48; Courtesy of David Clemo, pages 13, 55–56, 58; Courtesy of Noel Campbell, page 30; Courtesy of Shelley Ross, page 89; Courtesy EMI Music/Capitol Records—"Galveston" cover, page 122.